HP 41C CALCULATOR REPAIR

CONTENTS

PREFACE

HP started production of the HP41 family of handheld calculators at the end of 1979 and kept it in production until 1991. Such long production time span is testimony to its quality and adequacy to the work of engineers and scientists all around the world.

Many of us had a HP41c at its day, or lusted for one, and you've given yourself that gift. But one day you pick it up from the drawer, or it falls to the ground, and it doesn't start anymore. You are used to working with it, and you cannot imagine yourself using any other make. You swear by RPN and cannot use another calculator. You don't want to spend north of 140€ to get another unit. What do you do, then?

Repair it!

Unlike modern calculators, these units were designed to be repairable (for the current calculator models, HP service department just exchanges your defective unit for another new). But unlike previous HP models that seemed to be built as a tank, the HP41 different versions have some design "flaws" that cause many units to require repair even when properly maintained.

At The Calculator Store we are HP calculator fanatics, and the HP41c occupies the warmest place in our heart. Over the last years we have repaired many units, and we think that we have seen most of the problems that affect these machines. We do not claim to have found the solution for every problem, but we do have for most of them. Our conclusion is that 90% of the calculators we have seen can be repaired easily. And what's best: as most of the problems in the calculator are of mechanical nature, you do not need to know electronics to perform any of the repairs in this book.

While by all means the HP41 is a computer, this book will focus on hardware, not software; and we have done our best to avoid any electronics discussion. You will not see any equation, and only very few instructions to key in. We will mention some books and websites that address all these in the references at the end of the book.

For some of the issues described in this book, we have found not just one, but several possible solutions. We will describe them in the order we would use them, from the easier, less intrusive method to the more complicated procedure – based on how damaged your calculator is. In some cases, we will have to use specific parts, but many of the repairs can be performed without them.

Skills required will be kept to a minimum. Unless you need to change a screen, you will not require a soldering gun or any other "complicated" tool. For some repairs you will need a Dremel or similar small rotatory tool. But in most of cases the repair is simply a mechanical endeavor.

We are constantly refining the methods and parts shown in this book. You can access our website for the latest parts and methods – and you can ask us for any repair question at sales@thecalculatorstore.com.

Now let's start by knowing some things about our calculator.

1. THE HP41C FAMILY OF CALCULATORS

Some History

Hewlett Packard's calculator history is one of the most interesting endeavors of the twentieth century. You can read about it in "Bill and Dave" from Moses Malone[i] [ii]. From the first desktop scientific calculator, the HP9100, and later the first handheld calculator, the HP35, there were incremental improvements and sophistication in every new calculator along the way, leading to the HP65 and HP67 calculators, which had up to 4 functions per key, LED display and card reader. These were the kings of the LED era. There was no more possible advance on that direction: going forward, there would be more functions than key combinations; and a display with just numbers would not be enough in face of increasingly complex programs.

The HP design team in Corvallis, Oregon, set several new requirements for the new calculator:

- It had to be alphanumeric
- It had to use LCD, to reduce consumption
- It had to be expandable – both with peripherals and RAM/ROM
- All the keys should be re-programmable with functions or programs (as opposed to the previous calculators' "function keys")

It ended up being the most successful scientific calculator ever made. It hit the streets on July 16, 1979, and it was immediately the gadget everyone wanted – very much like the latest iPhone when there was nothing else.

Special features

The HP41C brought two features that made it different at the time: the alphanumeric display (made of segments, against the competing technology of dot matrix) and the expandability through the back ports.

A short time after, Sharp introduced the 1211 Basic computer, which was programmable in Basic and had a full dot matrix 1-line screen. Still, for most of us the HP41 was the calculator to have. Easy and fast to program, HP created a wealth of expansion possibilities, both in hardware and software.

The software expansion was mainly done through modules to be plugged in the back of the calculator. A never complete but quite extended list of available software modules is in appendix 2.

Serial number and places of production

HP used then a consistent method to assign serial numbers to their calculators. The serial number indicated when and where the machine was produced. It is located in the back of the calculator, on the upper right side.

The code was in the form YYWWCXXXXX, where the digits are:

YY : year of production, counting from 1960: 19 = 1979, 20 = 1980, 21 = 1981, etc.

WW : week of production. The earliest machine known to me is 1916 – owned by Richard Nelson. (In general, keep any 19WW machine – it is a vintage collector's item!)

C : country of production; A = USA, B = Brazil, S = Singapore

XXXXX : unit under that year, week and country.

Beware: the serial number is on the back side of the calculator. Someone repairing his calculator may have used parts from different calculators to assemble a good working unit: screen, front and back. HP used to replace damaged back sides with new ones without serial number – I have seen several of them.

Peripherals

From the beginning, HP introduced several peripherals that could be used with the HP41C

- The HP82104A card reader (we will devote a chapter to its more common repair)
- HP 82143A printer
- HP 82153A Optical wand (to read barcoded programs)
- HP 82242A infrared printer interface (to be used, for example, with the HP82240A/B printers
- The HP-IL loop and linked peripherals.

The HP-IL loop

The HP-IL interface was a ridiculously slow interface loop (typically 7 kbaud with two devices, less with more devices in the chain) that could handle printers, data storage and up to 30 peripherals, addressed automatically:

- HP 9114A/B Disc Drives
- HP 82161A Tape Drive
- HP 82162A Thermal Printer (mechanically equal to HP 82143A printer for HP-41C)

- HP 82163A/B Video Interface
- HP 92198A 80-Column Video Interface (Mountain Computer)
- HP 82168A, 92205M Acoustic Couplers (Modems)
- HP 82905A/B Printers
- HP 2225B ThinkJet Printer
- HP 7470A Graphics Plotter (Opt. 003 HP-IL Interface)
- HP 2671A/G Alphanumeric Graphics Thermal Printer
- HP 3468A multimeter

You may find some of them in the auction sites. I have been using a HP3468A multimeter and use the HP41C to program readings over time. Slow – but you don't need the speed! It just gets the job done.

2. IDENTIFY YOUR HP41

C, CV and CX

The initial model produced by HP was the "C" version (for continuous memory). It had 63 registers of memory, to be shared between data and programs. This soon proved to be too little for the kind of applications that the HP41 could do, so HP launched memory modules to increase RAM (each module included 64 registers), a QUAD Memory module (which had 256 registers), and finally the CV version, which integrated the memory in the board and reached the maximum 319 registers.

Later the CX model came out. Apart from the full register set of the HP41CV, it included a time module and a new type of memory: the extended memory, and a set of functions to use it (as well as other useful functions). This extended memory could not be used in the same way as the "main" memory (for example, programs could not be run from extended memory), but it allowed the HP41CX to reach 919 registers (by adding 600 extended memory registers to the previous 319 maximum)

You can differentiate these three basic models by the front label. Also, the C has a white rectangle encircling the keyboard (grey in the very early ones), while the CV and CX have it in yellow.

In general, the repair methods and parts are common to all three. For the sake or repair, the next division is far more important

Full nut and half nut

Initially, based on the technology of the moment, the calculator had a keyboard circuit, to which the screen was soldered, and a processor circuit, linked to the keyboard by a couple of zebra connectors between both. This version was called "full-nut", since the code for the calculator was "Coconut". All three above versions (C, CV and CX) were built in full-nut form.

It is worth noting that in the beginning, the main circuit was pressed to the keyboard circuit by a couple of nuts screwed to the screw posts. In later models, the circuit was pressed by two cylinders in the back of the calculator – which made the assembly more fragile. We will come back to this later.

Later in the HP41 life there was a full internal redesign, where the PCB technology was moved to surface mount and everything was put in the keyboard circuit. These new calculators were launched on 1985.

Here are pictures of the innards of both calculators:

Full nut:

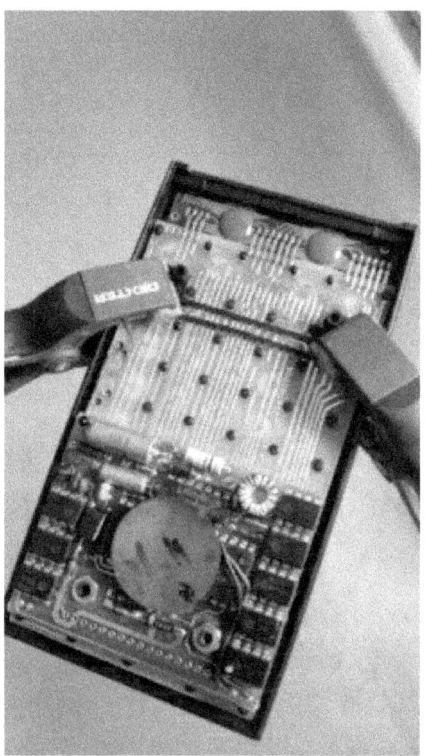

Half-nut (once retired the black plastic covering the circuit)

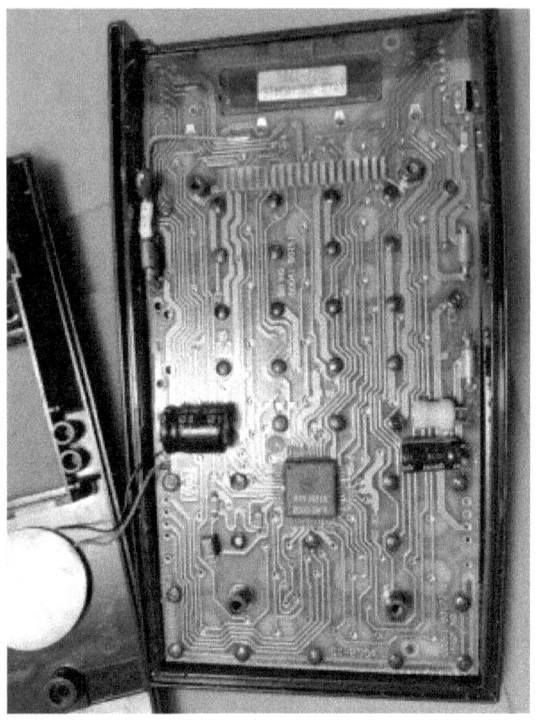

Far more integrated, with all processing power into a single chip below.

The way to distinguish them from the outside is the screen: the full-nut has a screen with square corners while the half-nut has rounded corners.

Full-nut screen:

Half-nut screen:

What is the importance of this? The half-nut units are far more reliable (since they have less failure modes and parts); but when they fail, they are more difficult to fix (akin to most current HP calculators). Many of the repair methods apply only to full-nuts; other methods are common to both types.

On the other hand, most HP41 devotees prefer the clearer segments of the old Full-nut model.

Tall keys and normal keys

The very first units (until mid-1980) had taller keys, with similar shape to that of the old HP65 and HP57 units. These are considered to have better touch than the later normal keys, and therefore the calculator is usually more valued (all other things equal). All tall keys are Full-nuts. They usually have an uneven touch on the 1 and 2 keys.

A tall-keys keyboard:

A normal keys keyboard:

There are also more differences between the tall keys and normal keys units. In the tall keys' units, the processor circuit is pressed to the keyboard circuit through nuts secured on the screw posts (self-threading). While it worked perfectly, you could not undo and redo the nuts many times, because that would break the thread.

The back side has flat supports for the lower screw pair:

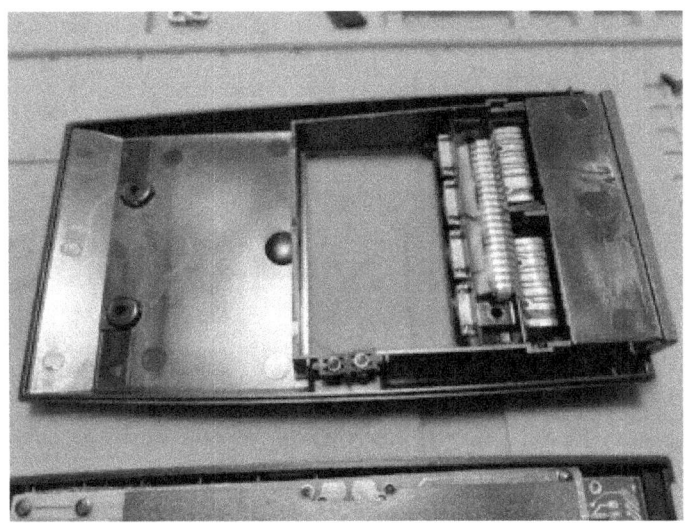

Here is a processor secured with nuts:

The later units had a couple of rings in the back side, which performed the pressure function, but then that made the two lower screws critical for the calculator to work: as soon as the thread wears out, the pressure on the zebras is insufficient and the calculator doesn't work. For many of us this was too much of a simplification and made the calculator less reliable and more prone to breaking.

Picture of lower screw supports with the added rings which provide pressure between boards:

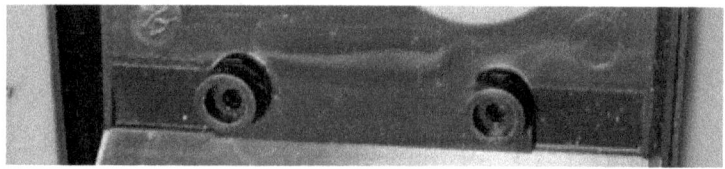

Screen revisions

The Full-nut HP41 had several screen revisions. We can skip a lot of classifications because broadly we can reduce it to two: the initial, square-driver-housing unit, and the following ones, with round-driver-housing. The initial set stopped being installed around serial number 1952AXXXXX, so if your calculator's is later than this, you can forget about it.

In general, full-nut screens are interchangeable, except for the initial set, which requires an additional capacitor to keep the switch-off time correct. We will return to this on the chapter devoted to screen fixing.

Screen pre-1952AXXXXX: note the square covers of the display drivers and the use of an additional pin on the left side of the screen connectors.

Screen post-1952AXXXXX: note the round epoxy covers of the display drivers. Just three pins on the left side (although there is a pad for a fourth)

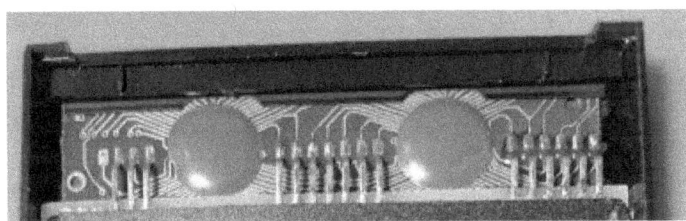

Metal keyboard surface

The earlier HP tall-keys (around the same date as the 1952AXXXXX units, but I have not proof for that date – in any case, the very early units) had also a metal top plate in the keyboard. Later it was replaced by the textured plastic surface that was used until the end.

You can see here the difference: the right one is the metal plate unit. It is less textured, more satin.

But attention: it is extremely easy to damage it when cleaning it or dropping any liquid on it. Any friction on that surface and the black paint disappears! Many wonderful units have been ruined by this problem. In particular, Deoxit or similar solvents destroy the paint coat – even when applied on the keyboard circuit inside!!

Also, this paint cover sometimes looks cracked, or dirty. But trying to clean it will only make it worse.

Otherwise, a magnificent surface that looks wonderful when in good shape!

Special models

It is worth noting that there was a "Blanknut" model for all categories (C, CV and CX). In it, the keys had nothing written on top, except the numbers and four basic arithmetic operators, as well as the blue letters on the slant part of the key. These units were designed to be completely customized (since all HP41 keys were re-assignable). These units are very sought after and can collect a high price on the auction sites. Functionally and mechanically they are identical to full-labelled units.

Full nut different circuits: in the appendix there are indications to distinguish the most frequent full nut circuits (in particular, C from CV from CX versions).

3.   TOOLS AND PARTS

We'll list some of the parts that we'll have to use in most of the repairs. There are some others which are "nice to have" or which it doesn't make sense to have for just one repair.

Tools - Required

- Philips-type screwdriver – different sizes
- Tweezers – short nose
- Tweezers – curved nose
- Small brush
- Small pliers
- Kitchen paper
- Caig DeOxit
- Magnifier glass
- Lens cleaner and microfiber cloth
- E6000 glue – black or transparent
- Documentation: HP41c Service Manual[iii]
- Soldering gun (for any screen related issue – not needed otherwise)
- Set of N-type batteries. You will need at least a couple of sets available – many failure modes can have high consumption.
- Conductive ink pen or conductive paint (only needed in case of corroded circuit traces)

Most of these tools are general purpose and will not harm by being in any toolbox.

Tools – nice to have but not required

- HP41c Service ROM
- HP41cv/cx service ROM
- Polywatch to repair scratches on screen
- Caig Pro-Gold
- Plastic welding glue
- Multimeter.
- Oscilloscope
- USB Microscope
- Extension module

Some comments to the parts list:

Contact enhancers

Caig DeOxit is a contact cleaner. It is miles ahead from any other we have used and leaves no residue. It really destroys rust and corrosion with a few strokes. It is expensive, though. It is used to remove corrosion and to clean unresponsive keys. If you have corroded lines in the main circuit, you will thank us for having recommended the Caig DeOxit and saving your calculator. Also, it can be used in any other electronic device that has corrosion, and to clean hi-fi and video connections (audiophiles swear by it, to perform a bi-yearly connection cleaning). In order to dissolve corrosion, is better to use the 100% version instead of the D5 (5% version). It comes in a variety of formats – we prefer the small needle plastic bottle.

Caig pro-gold is a different formulation that improves conductivity of contacts and protects from corrosion. It is to be applied after a thorough cleaning with Caig DeOxit has been done and will protect your connections for a long time. Same observations apply – including using it to protect connections elsewhere at your home.

Glues

We have tried several glues, and so far, we have settled on

E6000. It keeps some flexibility, and is resistant to vibration and hits, so it doesn't break. This glue is often used to fix jewels to their mountings. We use it to fix our screw posts replacement onto the keyboard circuit.

Cyanoacrylate is NOT recommended for the HP41c plastics. On the other hand, many people swear by solvent-based welding glues, also used in plastic models, like Tamiya extra-thin (part number 87038) or Revell Contacta (39604 or 39608). The HP41 plastics are "low energy" and it is quite difficult for them to react with solvents and have a permanent bond. In some formulations an "activator" should be used first on both surfaces. These glues should be used mainly on the upper screws supports in the back side of the body. However, this will continue to be a weak point and other methods are advisable instead.

Conductive inks

When the circuit traces are corroded, there are several paint solutions that can be applied with a brush; however, you need to have a steady hand and there is always the risk of spilling it over other things, as well as painting where you shouldn't.

Lately I have discovered a pen solution called Circuit Scribe. You can find it in Amazon. You need to write with it several times until you cover well the old trace. (The brush method would be faster, but also take longer to dry.) It is the method that I use now.

Cleaning

Many repairs require cleaning, and the first idea is to use the cotton swabs that you can find anywhere. However, in many cases they leave lint and therefore complicate electrical contact. It is better to use lint-free lens cleaner or microfiber lens cleaner, which leave no lint. This is key for screen repairs (which leads to a very unprofessional result with a dirt screen after all your hard work) and for connection cleaning – where a lint accumulation can lead to poor connection or no connection at all.

Documentation

The HP41C service manual[iv]. It is important to have a version with all the addenda – which in some cases is more important than the original document. The version referenced below includes all the addenda. Of course, for free!

Other tools

Service modules:

There are two types: for C and CV/CX calculator. They are not compatible with each other if they are to be used properly. A working replica can be obtained from Systemyde[v]. These are required to fully test the calculator, but we'd only advice to buy them if you're going to repair a lot of HP41!

Oscilloscope.

Just used to test when screen is not working, and we don't know if the calculator is on. To be used together with the extension module. Many of them have voltmeter and other measures, so it can be the core of any electronics workshop. They can be found second hand for limited amounts of money; however, its use for our purpose is limited.

Multimeter.

We do not really need an expensive, full-featured multimeter. We will use within this book basically as continuity tester (i.e. to check if a circuit trace is continuous or it is broken). To do that, it needs to be put in the diode-beep position (see picture below)

Spare Parts – replacement parts

We have developed some repair parts in flex circuit or HP Multi Fusion 3D printing technology.

- Battery module – assembled
- Battery flex circuit

- Battery holder with springs
- Replacement springs for battery
- Zebra connector - assembled
- Lower post repair
- Upper post repair
- Zebra holder
- Back side screw support repair
- Side port
- Back port
- Screws for upper and lower posts

They will be introduced on the respective chapter. Only required in specific repairs.

4. MODES OF FAILURE (OR TYPICAL PROBLEMS IN HP41C CALCULATORS)

The first HP calculators (often called "Classic": HP35, HP 45, HP55, HP80, HP65 and HP67) were very solid and well designed. The body was independent of the circuits, and the screws that secured the circuit were not required to hold the machine together too. This design resulted in very robust calculators. The HP41c, with all its technical advances, was not as robustly designed as the calculators that preceded it (with the exception of the Spice series, which was a true design flop). We have identified several weaknesses that appear again and again, and we have found solutions for them.

Types of failures

- Corroded battery contacts
- Broken upper back case screw head supports
- Broken upper screw posts
- Broken lower screw posts
- Corroded or broken zebra contacts
- Corroded circuit traces
- Damaged screen - black spots
- Damaged screen - not all segments light on
- Dirty screen

- Damaged plastic protection
- Damaged Keyboard

How to determine what is your problem? Beware - you may have to disassemble your calculator!

Corrosion on the contacts is very easy to spot. You can see the battery contacts corroded. It is usually the leftmost contact which gets corroded first. This is the lowest potential point ("-" contact of the set of batteries). Go to chapter 6

Broken upper back case screw head supports: you can see both halves of the case are loose in the upper part of the calculator. This impedes power transfer from the battery to the circuit. If you take the upper rubber feet out with a small flat screwdriver, taking care of taking the adhesive sheet with it, you see the screws below. You will be able to see that they are "free" in this case, or cracks or pieces on the plastic below. If they are not free, then the problem may be that the upper posts are broken - and you'll need to disassemble the calculator to see it. Go to chapter 10

Broken lower screw posts: the lower part of the calculator seems loose, and it may happen that it works when applying pressure to the lower part of the calculator keyboard (around keys 1, 2 and 3). In some cases, this cannot be seen immediately, but when removing the lower screws: they feel loose. Go to chapter 8

Broken upper screw posts: one or two of the upper screw posts is broken, or the screw thread broken. These screws are always under tension, since their function is to press the battery-ports module zebra connectors against the keyboard circuit. It can be seen because there is a gap between the calculator both halves in the upper part. It is possible that the calculator only works when applying pressure to both halves to close the gap. Go to chapter 9

Corroded or broken zebra contacts: you can only see it if you open the calculator. Indicators of this problem may be missing digits or segments in the screen, or the calculator not working, or discontinuous output on the screen. Go to chapter 7

Corroded circuit traces: you can only see it if you open the calculator. Usually happens with battery contact corrosion - never comes alone! Go to chapter 10

Damaged screen: in all cases disassembly is required.
- black spots: seen in the screen. You can only change the screen (soldering required!)
- not all segments lit: it can be the connections to the screen, the lower zebra corroded, the lower screw posts broken, etc.
For screen issues, go to chapter 11

Dirty screen: you can try with pressured air through the side openings, and if it doesn't work you will have to unsolder the screen.

Damaged plastic protection: complicated! sometimes the damaged plastic protection is easy to take off the machine; you need to disassemble and unsolder the screen; if it doesn't separate easily, we have not found yet a way to repair it. However, small and medium scratches can be removed – see chapter 11

Damaged Keyboard. There are three typical problem levels: keys not bouncing easily, keys broken and keys not working. There are several strategies, from light to heavy surgery. For the heavy surgery, we'd recommend avoiding it and buy another calculator: this is the most cumbersome and difficult repair in this book. But if it needs to be done, go to chapter 12

There are less frequent problems, for example errors in the processor module in the full-nut units. These seldom get damaged – maybe 1/100 of them require service. Our advice is NOT to repair them, but buy a replacement. A tested C circuit costs 10€ plus shipping (In case you have a defective HP41c circuit, you can take the opportunity to exchange it for a CV circuit (with 4 times the memory) for around 35€, or, much better, a CL circuit. For the latter, go to chapter 14.)

5. OPENING AND CLOSING THE CALCULATOR

Opening

The calculator is secured by 4 Philips screws, located underneath the 4 rubber feet. To remove these, use a small flat screwdriver. For the lower feet, start by the upper inner side (where the screw is). For the upper feet, the screws are centrally located so you can start wherever you want.

Unscrew slowly: these screws have been there for close to 40 years, and now the plastic is brittle and can break if handled roughly. The screws are self-threading, and the screw posts can only handle so many threads before becoming loose.

Once the screws have gone out, pull the calculator backside up vertically. Separate the middle plastic piece and put aside. Be careful of pieces that may fall, in particular the battery-ports module, or the springs and balls of the power connector.

Closing

Put the calculator keyboard face down. Place the middle plastic piece making sure that the "open" part is facing upside:

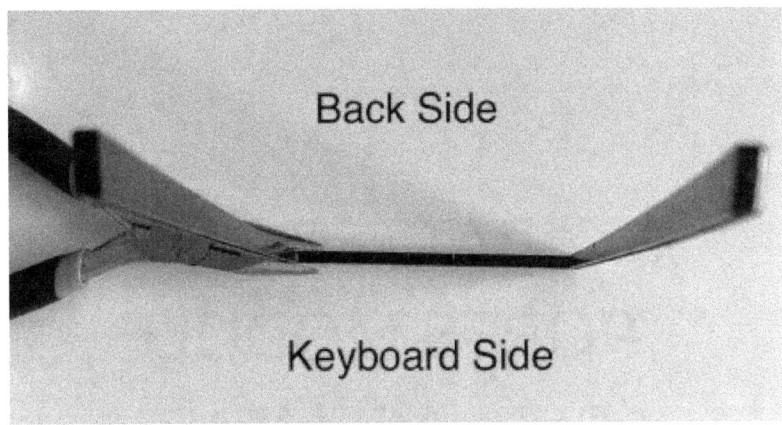

Put the module covers in the port holes. This is important to ensure that the battery module is pressed well from the top of the calculator and lands exactly where it is supposed to (i.e, the zebra connectors).

If the calculator is a Full-nut unit (i.e., it has a separate processor module resting on the keyboard circuit), there are two possibilities:

1. The processor is compressed to the main circuit through nuts. Then the back side does not have compression requirements and screwing can proceed normally for all 4 screws (the short ones below, the long ones up)

2. The processor is not compressed by nuts. Then the back side has two small cylinders around the screw holes that exert that function. Make sure that the area surrounding the posts in the main processor is clear and with no cables. In some cases, due to thinner processor circuit, a couple of plastic washers are required.

Once screwed in again, introduce batteries with the battery case and test. The "MEMORY LOST" message should appear. This is always received with joy, despite the wording!

6. BATTERY AND PORTS MODULE REPLACEMENT

This repair is suitable for all types of HP41. This is, by far, the most common of HP41 failures and one of the easiest to solve.

Material required: battery and ports module replacement part (see appendix)

1. Open the calculator (see chapter 5 for instructions)
2. Remove the old piece

Now it is the time to remove the damaged battery-ports module. To do that, first remove all 4 module covers or modules; then pull the module vertically and carefully, since there are four plastic tabs in the calculator used to secure it, and it you do horizontal movements you can bend or break them. Yes, they have also became brittle after all these years!

Sometimes grit and grease have "glued" the old piece to the backside. It will be very difficult to remove it. Be aware that it is NOT glued by design - this is an unwanted effect of grease, grit and time. To remove the piece in this case, try pushing up with a screwdriver on the back-module connectors. Increase upward force until eventually it separates from the body. Clean the backside plastic with water and soap or a lens cleaner. It may happen that one or both of the screw supports are broken. You will have to repair it before you continue, with the broken back repair piece (vid. Appendix)

Once the backside is clean and free from the old battery module, insert the new one carefully, making sure that the 4 vertical tabs are not bent. This is done without the module covers in yet. Be sure that it goes down to the calculator body. No light should be seen between both.

After it has been installed, put the module covers or modules so that they push the piece in place.

3. Reassembling the calculator (see chapter 5 for instructions)

Please be sure to eliminate rusting from the main board with Caig DeOxit (best), WD-40 or 3-in-1 for electrical contacts (not as good) or other suitable cleaner, applied with a micro-fiber cloth (best) cotton buds (usually leave fibers behind).

7. ZEBRA REPLACEMENT

This piece is for repairing only HP41c full nut calculators, substituting the damaged or corroded zebra connector that links the main board with the processor circuit. Our latest design is in a single piece, with 50 times more conductivity than elastomeric contacts.

Installation instructions

1. Open the calculator (instructions in chapter 5)
2. Remove the processor.

There are two possible cases:

- In the old calculators the processor circuit is pressed down to the main circuit by a couple of nuts screwed on the plastic posts. The posts do not have any thread themselves - the thread is carved by the nut itself. These have to be removed with care because you risk breaking the post, by unscrewing counterclockwise. More than a couple of "ins and outs" and the post will break for sure. Once unscrewed, lift the circuit.

- In the newer ones, from mid-1981, this pressure is exerted by two cylinders around the screw holes in the back side of the case. These are not present in the old models. You just need to lift the circuit.

Once the circuit is lifted, you will see the zebra connectors. These may be of three different types:

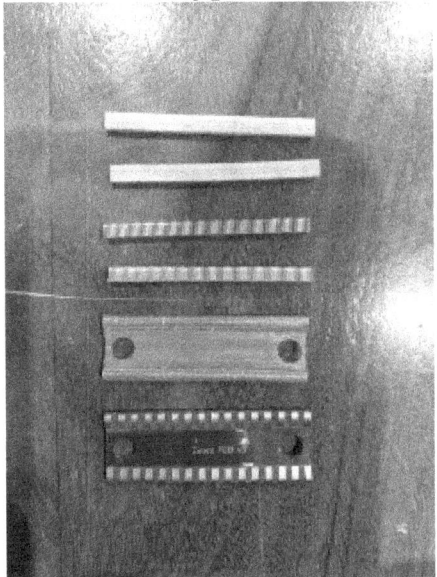

- The first pair is completely useless and will need to be replaced. Every time.
- The second one can be reused if treated with care and not corroded - clean it with paper embedded in Caig De-Oxit. However, it doesn't work in some circumstances and there is no clear reason why.
- The third type is the best of the lot and can be reused with care if not corroded. It is also sensitive to friction and can be easily damaged. Discard it if corroded.
- The fourth is the current alternative[vi]. Suggested to replace the first two versions.

Now you have to lay down the new zebra. As it is symmetrical, it works all 4 ways, in principle, but due to the way it has been made, it is better to lay it down with the lettering up, visible. Make sure it goes down to the end of the posts on both sides. All circuit traces should line up perfectly with the circuit pad below. Once laid down the zebra, put the processor circuit on top and press down to ensure contact.

If there is no more repair to do, you can close the calculator. (Usually, there is more to do...)

For the cases where there were nuts, we recommend not using the nuts anymore and replace them by one of our spacers. Nuts were a perfect solution 30 years ago; now it can contribute to break the weak, brittle plastic of the screw posts.

You can try several spacer height sizes until you find the one that closes perfectly the calculator and yet pushes down the circuit to ensure good contact. The exact height will depend on the main circuit you have and how high is the zebra you are using.

You can now reassemble the calculator according to chapter 5 instructions.

8. BROKEN LOWER POST REPAIR

This repair applies only to Full-nut units.

Material needed

- Lower post repair piece
- Clothes' peg
- Keyboard support for clothes' pegs

1. Open the calculator (chapter 5)
2. Alternative repair methods:

Let's assume that both posts are broken or cracked. The effect of this cracking is that the screws do not do their job. Depending on how broken the screw post is, we can do one or more of the below options.

Use longer screws.

Usually longer screws may help, but this typically is short lived since the cracks will continue downwards over time. Once the pressure between both halves is softened, the calculator doesn't work anymore (if it is not secured by nuts).

However, this solution may last for a long time and be enough if the posts were not too bad and the calculator is for your own use (I wouldn't do it for a customer). You can find longer screws here: http://www.thecalculatorstore.com/lower-post-long-screw-inox and here: http://www.thecalculatorstore.com/

lower-post-long-screw-black-pair.

Cyanoacrylate over the inner part of the post.

Another temporary solution is to apply cyanoacrylate glue sparingly over the inner side of the screw post and let it dry. You have a new flat surface where the screw may "bite" again a new thread.

It has to be a single coating and the glue has to be very fluid. Thick coatings will result in stressed post that will break sooner (sometimes immediately). Use a modelers' brush (or the brush that comes with some superglues).

You can combine options a. and b. for best effect too.

Broken post repair

The definitive solution is to repair the broken posts.

Old methods to repair broken post is to glue them (but this doesn't hold together too long) and to tie them down with very small gauge copper cable, applying pressure so that it holds together. This may solve some cases, but not when the screw thread has been destroyed - maybe due to strong tightening of the screws.

Other repair methods have been proposed, including drilling down the screw and placing in its place a metallic cylinder with screw path, glued in place. We tried this method but there was a problem: the torque used to secure the screw resulted in cracked glue and the cylinder separating from the substrate - every time, even with epoxy two-component glue.

Our method was devised with three goals in mind:

1. Try to avoid the torque from the screw forcing on the glue with the substrate
2. Try to ensure that the front part of the calculator is pulled up when screwing the back side on.

3. Try to be compatible with all known zebra connectors - including our own.

The piece that we have designed requires drilling the old posts to 3.5 mm below the keyboard circuit level, taking care of leaving the hole clear. The piece has two "grips" for the holes. These clip on the keyboard circuit, and expand when a screw is inserted, increasing the resistence to separation. The surface of the piece should still be glued to the keyboard circuit, so that the torque on the substrate is avoided (it also helps that torque is also resisted by the other post)

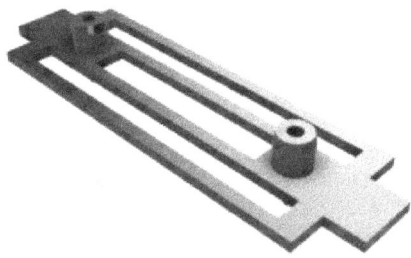

When gluing the piece, there are several precautions that need to be taken:

- Be sure of covering the zebra circuit part with tape - we don't want the glue to cover it.

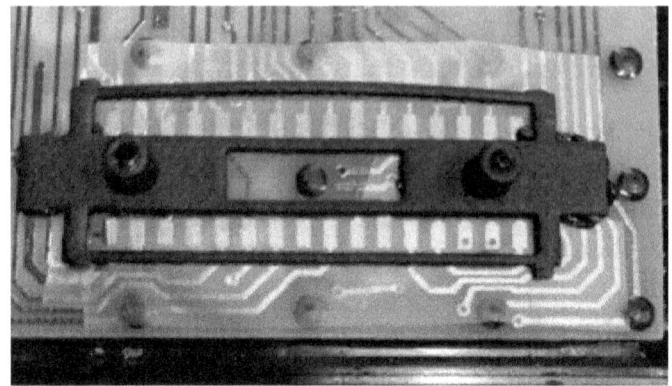

- Cover also all nearby pin holes of the keyboard. If glue comes into one such hole, the key will not register. In severe cases, the key will be down all the time, glued in place!
- When you position the piece, make sure of using some pins through the holes to make sure the piece is well centered, and the screws can go through.

- When applying pressure, use clothes' pegs to hold the piece in place, preferably on the outer side.
- To avoid pushing the keyboard down, and only push down the front of the calculator, use the keyboard cover we have designed to support the pegs. Pushing the keyboard instead will result on separation

between both halves of the calculator, since the attachment of the substrate to the pin will be at a lower level (the keyboard is linked to the keyboard circuit, not to the substrate). Alternatively, you can use a couple of credit cards which will avoid the clothes' pressing the keys all the time.

- Use E6000 glue. Make sure that there is no solvent or circuit cleaning residue – it will disable the gluing effect of E6000
- Let it cure overnight.
- Remove the tape over the zebra circuit trace: in particular what affect the circuit traces.

- Place the zebra connectors (if zebra connectors are damaged or corroded, go to chapter 8). Picture is from a replacement zebra connector

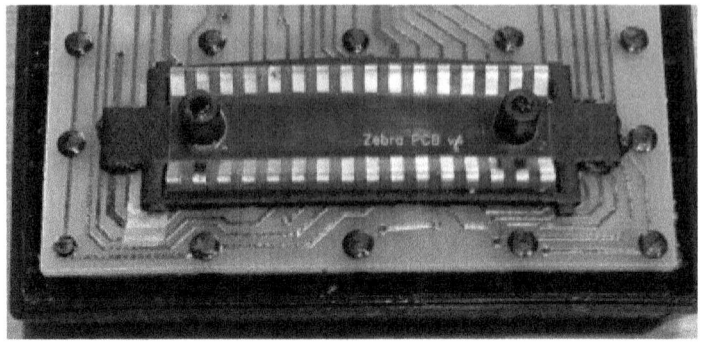

- Assemble the calculator and test.

We recommend repairing both posts at the same time. However, if you are confident on the resistance of the other post, you can cut the piece in two. As it is symmetrical, it can be used for both posts, just twisting it 180º.

Note: the repair piece has been given a couple of pads at the left and right, to increase the glued area and improve resistence to tension. In some cases, the solder points in the processor module may interfere with these pads, so the pressure needed between the processor and the zebra connections is transferred to the pad. We have seen several such cases, and it can be solved by filing away the tops of these solder points.

It also may happen in some extreme cases with the solder points between the two zebra connector lines. Our zebra PCB film is thicker than the original and more resistant, so it may also deflect some pressure off the zebra connectors, where it belongs.

In the following figure we show the solder point to carefully file away.

9. UPPER POST REPAIR

This repair applies to both Full-nut and half-nut units.

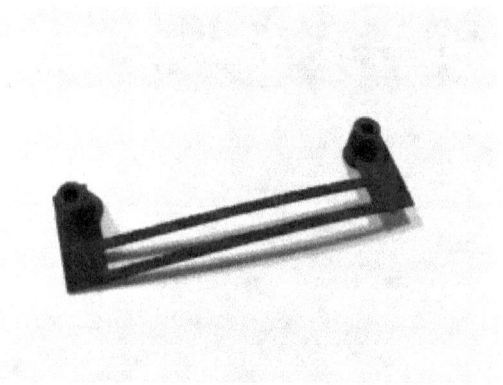

Material needed

- Upper post repair piece
- Clothes' peg
- E6000 glue
- Dremel drill (or equivalent)
- Scotch tape

1. Open the calculator
2. Post repair

Let's assume that both posts are broken or cracked. The effect of this cracking is that the screws do not do their job. Once the pressure between both halves is softened, the calculator doesn't work anymore.

An initial solution is to apply with a pencil a coat of superglue on the inner side of the post. This liquid enters in the gaps, covers the broken threads and in some cases will allow a screw to develop a new thread.

This will be enough in many cases! Close the calculator and test (calculator testing on chapter 13)

If this doesn't work, because the cracks are too big or the post is directly broken in pieces, the posts have to be rebuilt.

If the post has only lost the screw thread (i.e., the screw doesn't hold), but the post looks ok (no big cracks, no parts lost) you can try the following: with a cyanoacrylate glue (superglue) which has a brush for application, you can try to "paint" the inside of the screw post.

Beware of the brush bristles not entering the hole and painting onto the circuit, in particular on the zebra connection pads. This is difficult to see because superglue is transparent but prevents proper connection and the calculator will not work. If this happens, remove with a X-acto knife and utter care the glue droplets on the circuit. Clean it after with Caig Deoxit.

Old methods to repair broken posts is to glue them (but this doesn't hold together too long) and to tie them down with very small gauge copper cable, applying pressure so that it holds together. This may solve some cases, but not when the screw threads have been destroyed - maybe due to strong tightening of the screws.

Other repair methods have been proposed, including drilling down the screw and placing in its place a metal cylinder with thread, glued in place. We tried this method but there was a problem: the torque used to screw and unscrew resulted in cracked glue and the cylinder separating from the substrate - every time.

The piece that we have designed requires drilling the old posts to 3,5mm below the keyboard circuit level. The design on the piece is such that the cylindrical body will be glued to the rest of the screw post; and the surface of the piece can be glued to the keyboard circuit, so that the torque on the substrate is avoided (it also helps that torque is also resisted by the other post, when using the full piece)

When gluing the piece, there are several precautions that need to be taken:

- Be sure of covering the zebra circuit part with tape - we don't want the glue to cover it.
- Cover also all nearby pin holes of the keyboard. If glue comes into one such hole, the key will not register. In severe cases, the key will be down all the time, glued in place!
- When applying pressure, use clothes' pegs to hold the piece in place, preferably on the outer side.
- Try to place the other side of the pegs away from the keys of the keyboard – it may damage them permanently. You may use a couple of credit cards (or similar hard cards) to distribute the peg's pressure over a wider surface and the calculator corners.
- Use E6000 jewelry glue. We prefer black over clear just for clarity of repair.
- Let it cure overnight.
- Remove the tape.
- Assemble the calculator and test.

We recommend repairing both posts at the same time.

Alternatively, you can cut the other side of the 2-post piece with a tweezer and glue in place the rest of the piece.

10. BROKEN SCREW HEAD SUPPORTS

This repair applies to both Full-nut and Half-nut units.

As many units suffer from broken upper screw supports on the back side of the calculator, we have created pieces for the repair of the back side of the HP41C - which offer bigger surface for adherence and also serve to hold the battery assembly in case the little wings in the back side are broken.

Instructions: first method: back repair piece.

Parts required: Brokenback (http://www.thecalculatorstore.com/Piece-for-repair-of-back-case-of-HP41C)

11. Disassemble the calculator – see chapter 5

12. Be aware, before everything else, that the piece has a right side and a left side. This is due to the space for the tabs in the calculator that keep the battery-port

assembly in place. You need to be aware of this at all times - more so if you want to cut it as explained below.

13. Decide whether you will replace both sides or just one. The decision is easy when both are broken, but if one is not, you'll have to check whether the old standing support will withstand the pressure for long. Our recommendation is to replace both sides. If later one of the sides breaks down, the repair will be much more difficult and probably less solid. And you have already paid for both sides!!

14. If you are going to replace just one side, cut with a hobbyist scissors just the side you don't need, according to picture enclosed, again, be careful of cutting the side you don't need, since the piece has a single correct orientation! The rest of the piece will serve to increment the glued area, better align the piece in place and also to better support the battery-port assembly.

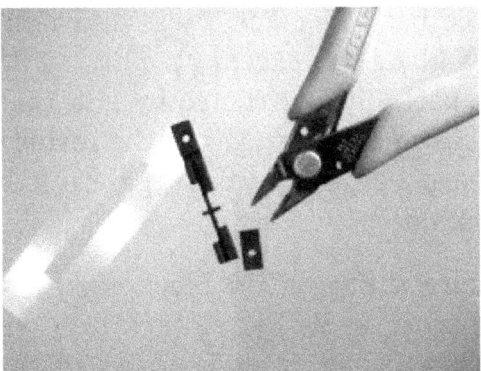

15. With a Dremel machine, file and level the area that had the support. You don't need to remove the tabs in between the two screw posts, but you need to remove them if they are twisted or half-broken.

16. Put the piece in place to check for proper fitting and adjustment. There is only one "right" way. The cross part is tight because it is needed to properly locate both holes at the extremes. Do not force it. Please make sure the piece is not bent downwards. Make sure it makes good contact. Remove the piece.

17. Put some glue in the bottom of the piece. Do not put too much or it will go out and spread around when pressed. We have used E6000 black glue with good results. Do not use cyanoacrylate glues. Put the piece back in place. Press and remove with a stick or a blade the excess glue, if any. If the screw holes are partially obstructed by glue, pass a screw in the opposite direction (from the inside to the outside of the calculator, to avoid separating the piece from the back side).

18. Secure the piece in place with a pair of clamps - lighter pressure like clothes' pegs will not be enough. Be careful that there is no excess glue from the other side of the case to avoid the clamps being adhered to the piece! Leave for 24h for the glue to cure. And you're done! You have a repaired back that will withstand a lot of abuse again.

19. The piece is designed to accept both the original and the new battery-ports assembly - so you need to press it down to have it in place. The screw holes should fit a little bit tighter than in the original calculator but should be perfectly aligned with the assemblies and the screw posts below.

Alternative Method: integral piece.

We have also designed a battery-ports module with a flat floor. This design is intended to replace the above part and glue the battery-port module in place. The advantage is that it holds better because there is a much larger area for adherence. The disadvantage is that it is a non-reversible repair: if it goes wrong, you have lost the backside of your calculator!

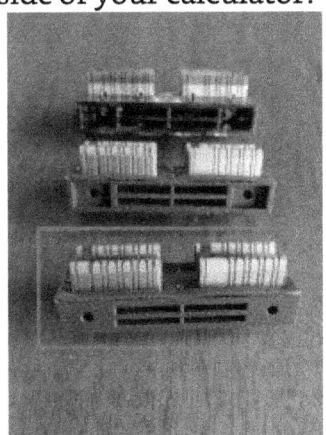

Same precautions apply, plus one: you need to be sure that it will work before gluing it in place.

After drilling down the broken old screw supports, position the piece in place, put all four port covers (or modules, as you may have), close the calculator without screws, secure with two strong rubber bands the upper and lower part of the calculator, introduce a fresh battery set and try it. This may be done in the other methods but in this case is more important – if the module is not working, gluing it will be a disaster!

All battery-ports modules are tested before shipping, but all calculators may have small differences in the exact position of the connectors, and some ports may not work. This is the moment to test it.

Once satisfied, you can safely glue it in place. Apply a coat of E6000 all around the base, including the horizontal holes in its center part – this will be used to further adhere to the base through the four little tabs – if they still exist.

The quantity is not as critical as with the previous method: the spilled-around glue will not obstruct anything – although it is easy to clean it with the tip of and x-acto knife before drying.

Place a couple of pegs on the flat sides rounding the holes. Make sure that the other side of the peg is not touching glue – or it will be adhered too.

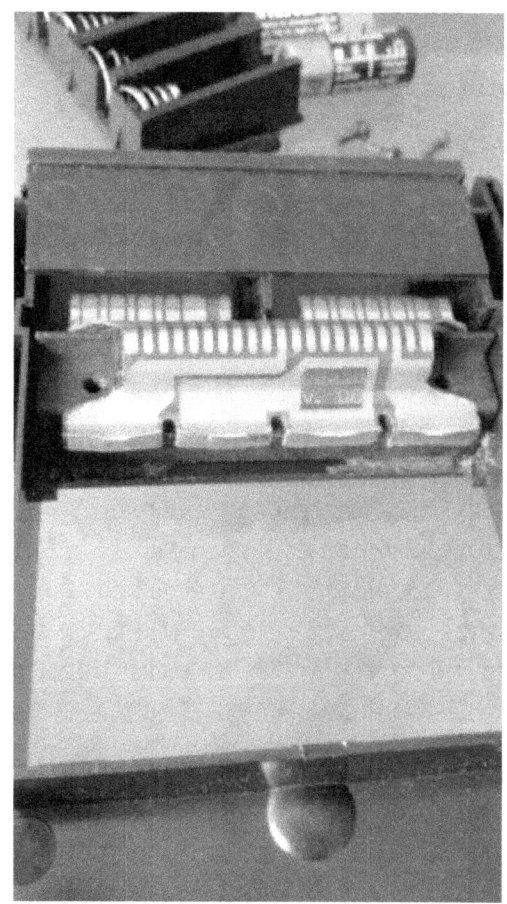

11. CORRODED CIRCUIT TRACES

Usually this problem happens together with a corroded battery contact, or with a corroded zebra. In some cases, there is just corrosion over the circuit traces. You need to put some drops of Caig DeOxit solution, let it soak the corrosion, and then remove it rubbing with a cotton swab until removed. Please take care with the rubbing, since you may remove the trace with it, depending on how serious the corrosion is, and whether it has peeled off the trace from the PCB surface.

This cleaning works for most of the times; but there are cases where the whole trace has disappeared, and the circuit will not work unless you complete the trace with conductive material.

The best solution is a conductive ink pen called Circuit Scribe. It can be found in Amazon and other outlets. You can draw with it on the PCB, and it will not spill around like a paint solution would. Please be sure of shaking it extensively before use.

Let the ink drawing dry before use. It will not be conductive until fully dried, so do not freak out if your continuity tester doesn't beep just after drawing.

This is an example of a very worn-off early HP41c that is converted to CL.

You can see here several traces painted with Circuit Scribe. Two of them are even contact points of the battery-ports module zebra connector – and it works fine!!

Incidentally, you can see also a surface-mount capacitor soldered between the pins of the screen. This happens with old screens, where the lack of it alters the time constant for the auto-off. More on this later.

12. SCREEN PROBLEMS

Warning: soldering iron may be required. If you are not comfortable, there are several guides in internet[vii]

There are several problems related to the screen. Some may be just cosmetical (dirty screen, black parts) and other prevent the proper use of the calculator. Many of them require the use of a soldering iron with a small tip – however, it is much easier that you may think. We will not discuss the use of a soldering iron – there are many tutorials in internet about it. Suffice to say that you will need a small tip, and you need to be fast with the iron because the connectors are small, and the same way you can unsolder the screen from the circuit, you can unsolder the connector from the screen if you maintain the heat long enough – and then it is much more difficult to solve it. So: keep the soldering iron hot, clean, and be fast!

Dirty screen

Or how to get out of the screen these "specs" or dirt accumulated over so many years.

There are escalating possibilities to clean the screen - depending on the difficulty in getting out the crud.

The first strategy is to try to move it out. For this you will need a keyboard cleaner - these sprays of compressed gas. It can easily be found in amazon or aliexpress.

The first way of using it is through the two open places in the back of the calculator. These holes are normally used to fir the latches of the card reader, but now they can serve our purpose. Blow compressed air through one of the holes and see if the dust or specs move out. Do not worry about the freezing that appears – it is just condensed water that will disappear very fast. Try also with the other hole just in case too. If that doesn't work, you will need to open the calculator. Beware - opening a calculator may mean that you break things that will require a full repair. You need to decide if it's worth trying. If so, follow chapter 5 instructions for opening and closing the case.

With the screen facing down, pull up the back-half case. Now you should be able to see the back of the screen. You need to try now to use the cleaner through the sides of the screen. This is closer to the goal than the back holes – it may work.

I usually stop there. If you really want to clean it more there are two options: bending the screen cables or unsoldering the screen. Both put the screen on risk - your call!

The safest bet is to unsolder the screen. First of all, remove the spacer piece that is at the top of the calculator screen. It is not glued, and you can take it out picking it with your fingers from its edges.

To unsolder the screen, you need to heat the connection on the keyboard circuit with a small tip solder iron, while prying up the connector lightly – one by one. Be fast, because if the connector is heated for too long, it can be unsoldered from the screen – and that is more complicated to resolder.

Important to repeat: the unsoldering must be done on the calculator circuit pads, NOT on the screen pads. The screen solder pads CANNOT BE soldered again - you lost your screen!!

Once unsoldered, pry the screen out by pulling from the openings at both sides, with a little twist since the screen goes slightly below the keyboard circuit. Avoid touching the LCD screen with your fingers, and avoid at all costs to damage the screen connectors.

Now you can clean the screen and the plastic protection, using lint-free lens-cleaner paper, wetted with lens cleaner. Do not use cotton swabs since they leave lint.

If the plastic protection is damaged, move forward to that part later in this chapter.

Screen repair

The LCD in the HP41C was the first LCD used by HP, and it was a real breakthrough at the moment. However, this was nearly 41 years ago, and it has been a long time since it was discontinued: there are no replacements except if we are able to salvage it from another defective calculator. Therefore, it is good that there are some problems that can be solved just by cleaning and fixing, as we will see.

The comments below apply only to Full-nut units. In the half-nut units, the screen is integral to the circuit and changes are not possible. We have not been able to repair half-nut screens.

There may be several issues with the screen:

1. Some segments cannot be seen. Once everything else in the calculator has been sorted out and cleaned, then it may be the screen. If there are only a few segments missing, or without a rule (the upper segments, etc.), this usually indicates a defective connection between driver and LCD.
2. Only half of the screen (left or right) displays symbols. This may mean that there is a defective connection, or that one of the display driver circuits is defective.
3. The screen only works when you press a key, and only while it is pressed. This usually means as well a defective driver circuit.
4. The screen only appears sometimes and not others.

However, the system is working as seen by a trace in the oscilloscope on the signals __ and __. This may be a bad connection of the screen – check all pins by pulling lightly with a tweezer.

5. The screen segments are lighter than normal.
6. There are black spots on the screen. This requires changing the LCD, which means another calculator... sorry!

When the screen does not allow all segments to be seen, it may be one of several faults:

- Bad connections of the lower zebras. The solution is to clean with contact cleaner the contacts in both circuit, keyboard and zebras; and if it continues to not work, then change the zebras.
- Bad connections of the lightly soldered screen pins. First you need to check with a flat screwdriver, pushing lightly all pins laterally, one by one. If any gives, then you will have to resolder it. A small solder will suffice. Normally there is no need to add more solder - the one already applied is enough. Make sure that contact is made by applying downward pressure to the pin with the flat screwdriver that you used to test it.
- Bad connection between the LCD and the screen driver. If the two previous steps have failed, you need to check this one to discard the last one. You need to:

  ◦ unsolder the screen, by prying softly with a plier while heating in the solder pad on the keyboard. Do not keep the heat for long or the driver will be damaged!
  ◦ Takin upmost care of not touching the screen connection pins, carefully pry out the upper and lower black metal clips that hold together the screen and screen drivers. Be very careful with the screen pins - it is very easy to bend them or

separate from the body!!

- ◦ separate the two halves (screen and screen driver) carefully. There is no glue between them: the only thing keeping them together is grit.

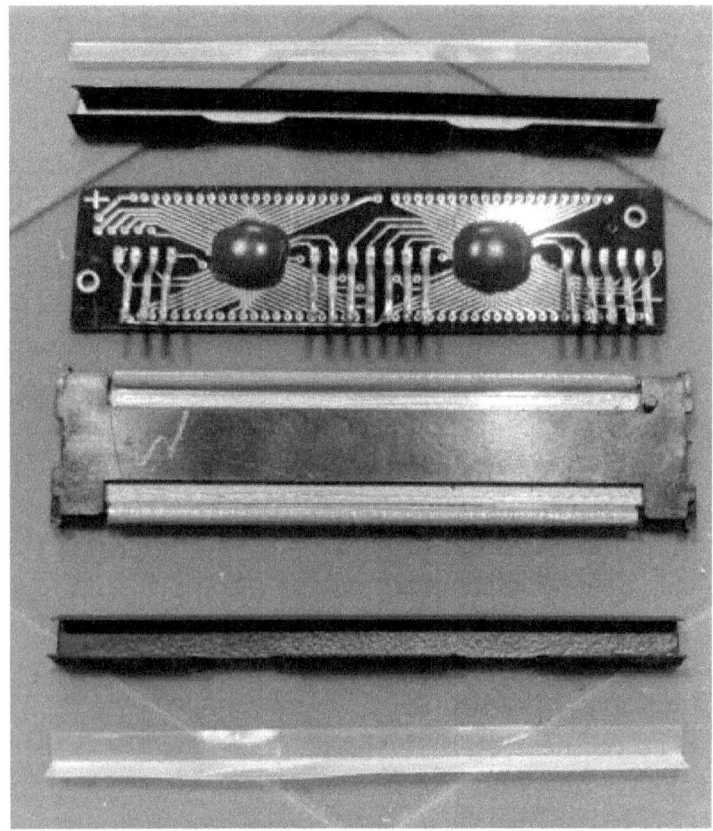

- ◦ There are two zebras, up and down of the screen. These zebras may be elastomeric or metallic. In both cases, clean them with a lint-free paper embedded in Caig Deoxit. You will be surprised at how black the paper comes, in case of the elastomeric connector! Do not use a cotton swab since it leaves fibers that will prevent a good connection. Repeat until paper comes clean. Also, clean other grit that you may see.
- ◦ Put both halves back together. There will be

only one possible position if you align the holes properly.
  ◦ Put back the clips. To do that, first make sure that the two plastic "L" are aligned and slightly out on one side, to facilitate the entry. Second, take care that the two dents are on the circuit side, not the screen's. Then, starting from one side, slide the clip over the screen. It will not be scratched since the plastic L should protect it. Be careful again with bending or damaging the pins! Once finished, do it with the other side. The plastic Ls are critical to maintain isolation and avoid damaging the screen.
  ◦ Solder back the screen.

-       One of the two screen driving circuits gone bad. This typically results on half of the 10 digits not working. This tends to happen when someone burns the circuit by inserting A24 batteries instead of N-type, subjecting the circuit to 48 volts instead of 6. The only solution is to find a donor machine and replace the screen. Use a small soldering gun and help lifting the pins with the tip of a plier, one by one. To solder the new one, follow the procedure in the above paragraph.

Damaged Screen Protection

After a lot of time searching, we have just found a good solution to repair your scratched HP41C screen. There is an abrasive product used to repair watches' plastic screens, called Poliwatch. You can easily get it from Amazon and other sources[viii].

The method: just apply a little quantity on the scratch, and then rub firmly with a soft cloth. You will get, once cleaned, a bright surface without scratches. If the scratch is too deep, you will need substantially more time – but it can be done. It is good policy to surround the whole screen with scotch tape to avoid spilling of the white matter – it takes longer to clean it and it may fall on keys!

Note: while you could use a Dremel to do it at minimum speed and with the cotton head, after some tests, we have found that the Dremel method can overheat the plastic and lead to internal cracks or material deformation that can be seen on the screen, rendering it unusable. It has to be manual!

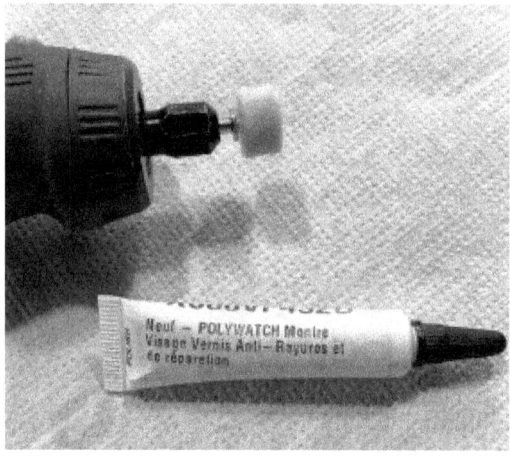

Beware: do not try to use this material on crystal - it is much harder than plastic and it would not help at all. This material is intended for plastic watches like Swatch and Casio. You'll be surprised how easy is to fix their screens too!

13. DAMAGED KEYBOARD

We will concentrate on the full-nut machines in order to fix the keyboard.

The typical problems we may have with the keyboard are three:

- Bad or no contact of some the keys.
- Mushy, soft feeling of the keys
- Keys slant (this is due to broken keys even if it can be seen from the outside)

The keyboard in the HP41c is composed of 4 parts:

1. The keyboard circuit, including the domes for the keys
2. A rubber protective surface
3. The keys themselves
4. The front side of the calculator (which is made of a plastic body and a sheet of other plastic material where the yellow labels are printed)

For the first and second problem, it is worth trying the following procedure before the extensive surgery we will discuss later.

Cleaning the domes from the back

1. Open the calculator (following chapter 5 instructions)
2. In case of full nut:

    a. Take out the processor

    b. Remove the zebra connector

3. Locate the dome corresponding to the key that doesn't work. It will have a small hole that connects with the interior of the dome

4. Put a drop of Caig Deoxit (preferably of the 100% version) in the hole and "remove inside" with a needle.

In many cases, this is enough to improve contact and key feel.

If the keyboard continues to fail, the next step is a "full cleaning" of the keyboard. This can only be done with full-nut units.

Full keyboard clean-up

1. Open the calculation following chapter 5 instructions.

2. Take out the processor

3. Take out the zebra connector

4. Find a small jar and fill it with water up to slightly

less of the height of the screen of the calculator. If the jar is transparent you will see what is happening, so it is recommended.

5. Put some drops of dish-cleaner – yes, the same one you use when hand-washing your dishes.
6. Put the calculator in it. The water SHOULD NOT REACH THE SCREEN. Keep it for 10' max. Remove the water with the calculator
7. In principle, the water should get quite dirty – VERY dirty in some cases.
8. Empty the jar, fill it with some fresh and clean water and remove all rests of soap.
9. Shake it all ways to take as much water as possible and let it dry.

If the procedure didn't work, you have always the "surgical" alternative below.

Full keyboard rebuild

To access the keys, we need to remove the keyboard circuit. For that, we need to remove the 50 plastic rivets that keep it in place. To that effect, we need to remove the heads of the rivets with a X-acto knife, one by one. Be careful with your fingers – the rivets break quite soon and the X-acto blades go into your fingers like butter.

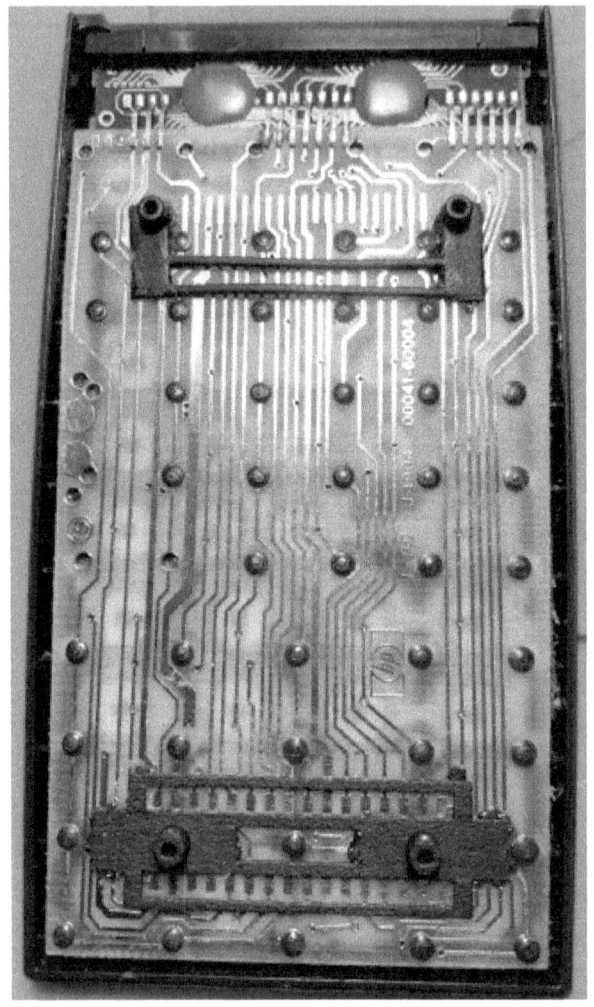

Once the 50 rivet heads have been removed the circuit can be pulled up.

Facing inside:

Facing outside (or to the keys). This is the part that has the mechanical action.

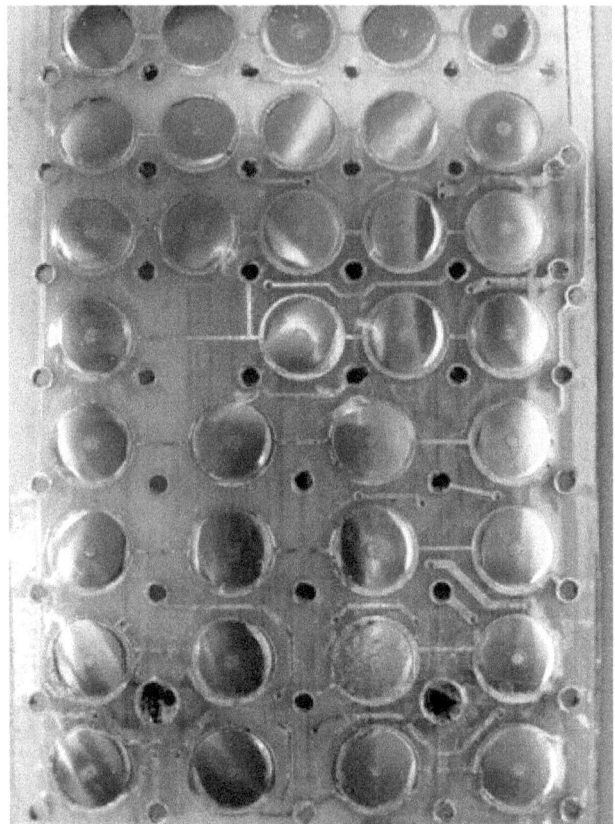

After it, there comes the protective rubber surface and then the keys.

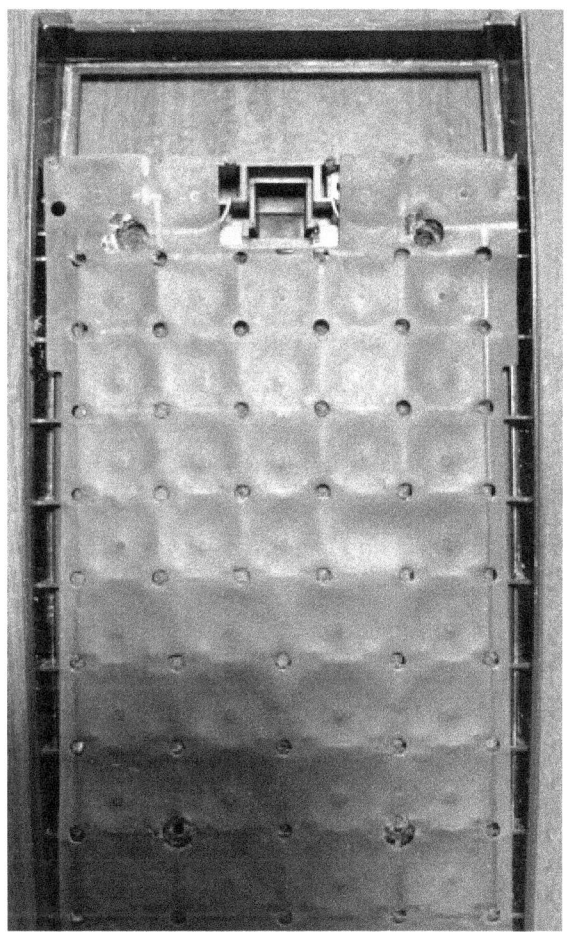

In most old units, the protective surface and the keys are full of debris and dust. The rubber surface must be cleaned with water and soap. Take care in removing all traces of corrosion from the circuits.

The keys can be cleaned with water and soap and a toothbrush (that you don't plan to use anymore!). Let them dry. Marvel also at the quality of these keys: the white of the lettering is NOT printed, but is the white plastic co-casted with the black material.

Now it is also the moment to improve the click and contact of the keys. In the keyboard circuit, locate the keys that were mushy or didn't register. You need to peel off the adhesive film that covers the whole side of the circuit. Its function is to keep the domes in place. Start peeling from the closest point to the defective key. Once you reach it, pull the dome open. You will find either dust or corrosion making the connection impossible or the bad clicking action. Once cleaned, put the dome and the film back in place, and test the click with your fingers.

Before assembling it back, check for any broken key. What usually breaks are the link between the rotation axis and the key. Glue it with E6000, using it sparingly. Our tests with cyanoacrylate glues have failed miserably, as well as with Revell welding glue for models. They just can't withstand the continuous stress of your keying.

To assemble back the keyboard, lay down the front plate, and then place the keys. Be careful when placing them since the positioning from your point of view is a specular layout compared with a normal calculator. Use this picture:

Do take care also with the top double buttons – it is very easy to put them in the wrong place too!

And here is how the keyboard would look while you're setting the keys (did you take the opportunity to clean all keys? Later it will be impossible!):

Now, before reassembling it, let's consider how to do it:

If the posts were ok, then you can assemble it with the old posts.

If either the lower or the upper pair of posts were broken or defective, this is the best moment to change them by collating the repair part (see chapter 9 and 10 respectively). Adhere them to the main circuit now. Be generous with glue – it won't spill down to the keyboard! Still, you need to avoid the holes, lest the glue comes into the domes.

Now you can reassemble it. First put the keyboard surface, then the keys (making sure of the position and that both sides of the "hinges" are in place), then the elastic surface, taking care of aligning the holes with the sticks left over from the rivets, and then the circuit, making sure that the domes are down, of course.

Now place either our keyboard protection part[ix] or a number of credit cards to distribute pressure, and place 6 pegs as seen in the picture:

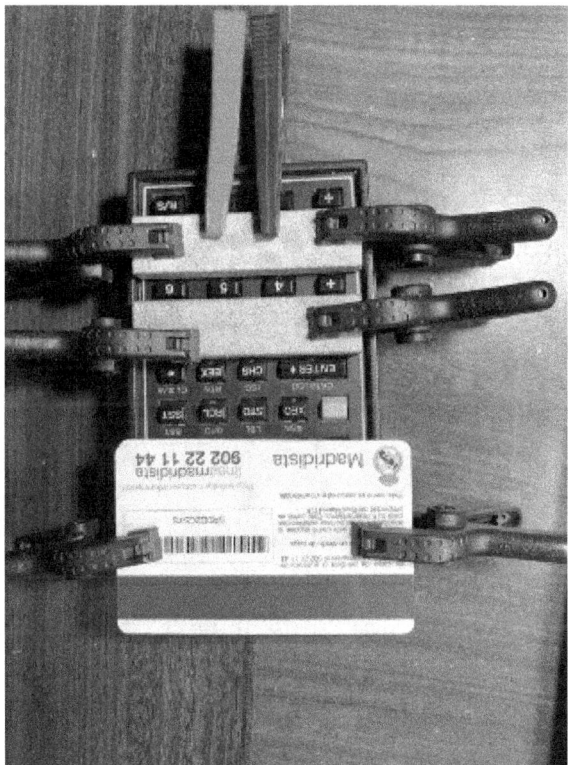

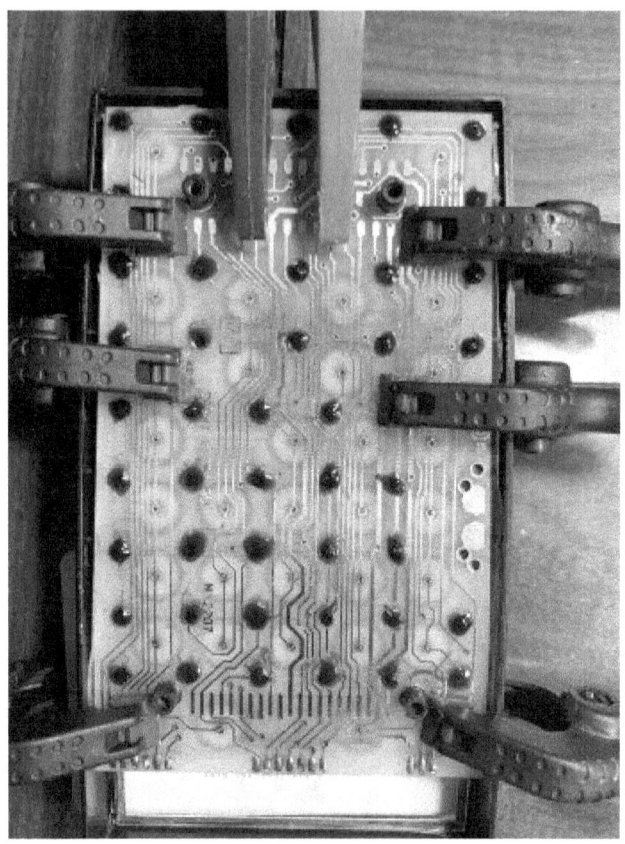

Now you need to place a drop of E6000 glue on each and every old rivet spot. If your E6000 glue doesn't flow easily, it is probably a little bit too old and you need to get a newer one. It is important that the glue flows well, so that it can penetrate around and in the holes of the rivets. Apply generously – the glue will shrink when it dries, and this shrinkage is welcomed: it will pull the keyboard against the circuit!

Let dry overnight. Test it the following day.

Do not worry if the keys "rattle" a little when you move the calculator – original HP41 used to do that, in particular tall-keys models; if they don't do it now, is usually due to the grit and mud that is preventing that movement – the same grit and mud you just removed.

You will have now a nice-to-the-touch action, perfectly working keyboard.

14. CALCULATOR TESTING

Now you have assembled the calculator and you need to check if everything works. When you assemble it and put the batteries, the best you can expect is to see the "MEMORY LOST" message. This happens when the processor has lost its power and the capacitors have been discharged. Nothing to worry about. (If there was still charge in the capacitors, you would see 0.0000 instead)

Test with a Service Module (C or CV/CX)[x]

There are different modules for C and for CV/CX calculators. Please use the one corresponding to your calculator.

I introduce the module in the lower left port, before introducing the batteries. The lower ports have the longer circuit – if they work, then the upper ports do, too.

When batteries are inserted, in many cases the service module initializes and tests the CPU. If it works you get to a screen to select the test.

HP41c

You need a "C" service module. I usually plug it first in port 4 (in the back of the calculator you will see which port is which), since it is the one to be used by the card reader and we ensure that way that both port 2 and port 4 work. After the complete test, we recommend inserting it in port 3 and start the test again. If it is recognized, then also ports 1 and 3 work.

Once you press the "on" button, a check of the CPU is performed.

Once the test is OK, press RS and you will arrive to a screen for test selection. For the automatic set of tests, press PRGM. Then the system starts checking the screen. You can see which segments are missing, if any. You will see here if any driver is failing, too:

First of all, all segments for a moment. Check for any missing.

Then, a couple of "S:" moving across the screen:

Then the @ sign at all positions:

Then the memory banks are tested. If they work, then you will get the "D/S OK" message:

After that, the ROMs are tested. The test circles through 0, 1 and 2, and can be seen in the flags being lit each time.

And then you get the OK (or a message with the wrong ROM ICs)

Next there is the is the keyboard test. You need to press the keys, one by one, from top left to bottom right. If some doesn't work, or you jump a key, the test will fail.

Once finished:

You need to press R/S to jump out of the test or Y if it failed or you jumped a key (or had a double-click on another)

Then the system tests the standby:

You need to have it for three seconds, and then press R/S. If it reactivates properly, you will have this message:

Then the system tests the auto-switch-off and switch-on. It should go blank and be only restarted by pressing the ON key. Any other should not work.

After this, you would have all the tests passed, or a message with the tests not passed. If the tests are not passed, you can check with us for solutions. For most of the failed tests, the solution will be changing the processor – unless you want a much more involved analysis of the processor innards; in other cases, the solution will be changing the display driver.

There are more detailed tests, which are out the scope of this book. To get to them, please read pages 103 to 108 of the HP 41c service manual – already linked elsewhere in this book.

HP41cv/cx

You need a CV/CX module. The process is the same, with a small difference: if your model is a CV, then you need to press PRGM for the automatic set of tests to start; if your model is a CX, press USER (so that the time module tests will be triggered too)

Test without Service module

If you do not have the service module, you can still perform a good number of tests. You will not be able to know for sure if the main processor is working well, but you can test it type "black box": if it behaves ok, then it is most likely ok! However, you will need a module of any kind in order to test the ports' connections.

1. Switch the calculator on. It should show "0.0000"

if it has been used before, or "MEMORY LOST" in case it has been without battery for a long time. (when repairing the HP41c, the above message is actually "good news"!). If it doesn't start, check the battery contacts for corrosion, but make sure also to check whether the springs in the battery holder are corroded – many a calculator perfectly functional has been discarded for this little item![xi]. Clean the contacts with Caig Deoxit or another suitable contact cleaner. For the springs, you can file them until corrosion is out. If the contacts are OK, then the problem lies elsewhere, and we'll have to open the calculator. If not, read on.

2. Test the "User" button. The "user" flag should appear on the lower part of the LCD. If it doesn't work, try harder. If it doesn't work still, the keyboard may need further cleaning.

3. Test the "Alpha" button. If it works and it sends you to a screen with no numbers, try pressing some keys and see whether they register at all. Then, clean the screen and write "*" until you fill the screen. This will give you a view on whether all the "internal" segments are working. (We will use the "8" to check for the external segments)

4. If you have modules, put them in the lower slots and check whether they are recognized:

    a. If they are memory modules, by executing XEQ SIZE 100 and see if it works or you get "TRY AGAIN".

    b. If they are other type, press CAT 2 and see whether the module is found or not.

    c. If the module is recognized in the lower slot, it will be recognized in the upper slot too.

15. NEW: CL MODULE INSTALLATION

Several years ago, the company Systemyde[xii] developed a circuit compatible in hardware and software with the processor in HP41 full-nut calculators. This circuit put 30 years' worth of improvements in electronics to our old calculator, bringing it to 2020. Its characteristics include:

- All features of an HP-41CX, included, if chosen, the Time Module.
- Full 600-register Extended Memory is built in.
- Over 300 plug-in module images are built in. Functions are included to allow these images to be virtually plugged into a calculator port and unplugged from a calculator port. You have in your hands the power and programs of all HP41 developers in your hands!
- Turbo mode, which allows the calculator to run at up to 50X normal speed. Actual values available are 2X, 5X, 10X, 20X and 50X.
- Several empty pages (4K in length) of Flash memory are available for non-volatile storage. You can store many calculator statuses, and you can bring them back with a command, giving you several different calculators in a moment.
- 122 pages (4K in length) of RAM are available.
- All RAM is continuously powered.
- A sophisticated Memory Management Unit (MMU)

allows full access to the large physical memory.

- Full bus compatibility for the Ports, allowing the use of any peripheral designed for the HP-41 system.
- A full-duplex serial port is available when the optional serial connector is used. This optional connector uses a 2.5mm stereo jack mounted in a blank port cover.

There are more detailed features and instructions in Systemyde manual[xiii], but we'd like to introduce you to this fantastic circuit and how easy it is to install it. Cost aside, we would not understand not trying to convert a C or a CV calculator to CL! The responsiveness of the calculator in all programs, and having all modules at your fingertips, changes the HP41c from a vintage toy to a modern, dependable, comprehensive tool.

There is a Wiki site devoted to the CL circuit.[xiv]

This circuit requires a full-nut HP41 calculator. You can identify it, as we discussed before, by the square corners of the screen. In most cases (except some units with serial number starting with 1954A or lower) it is a pure drop-in circuit exchange. (for the 1954A units a capacitor has to be soldered to two of the screen pins – see Systemyde instructions. We can provide the capacitors if needed)

Here is a picture of a normal screen circuit that can be used without additional fuss:

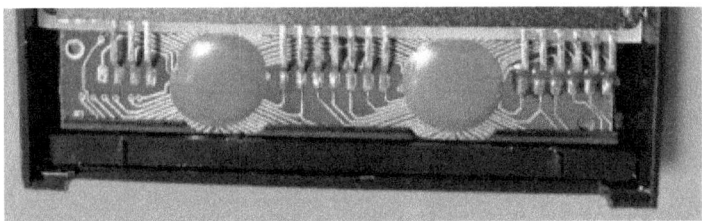

And here is a picture of the screen that requires a capacitor to be soldered. Note the square epoxy driver cover.

In order to assemble the CL circuit, there are very few and simple steps, compared with other repairs in this book.

First, make sure that you "donor" calculator is working. If not, you won't be able to know if something went wrong with the installation or it was an already existing problem.

Second, also before starting: make sure you treat the modules very carefully. You can burn them with and electrostatic discharge - so put your wrist to ground with some device. There is yet another precaution. necessary: there are many small cables and surface mounted components, which are much easier to break and destroy than the old components that were soldered through the circuit.

Instructions:

17. Disassemble the calculator. Go to chapter 5 for instructions.
18. Once disassembled, remove the old circuit. If the circuit is secured with nuts, you can unscrew them carefully with a pair of small pliers. If not (secured in place by the pressure of the small cylinders of the back side of the calculator), it is enough to pull it up carefully. put aside.
19. Check the innards, and clean all zebras with Caig DeOxit - both sides. Caig Deoxit not only cleans the connections from all rust, but also creates a protective film to it.
20. Put the CL module where once was the old processor.
21. If the old processor was secured with nuts, we do not recommend putting them back. It is very easy that the pliers or any other tool moves around and dislodges a capacitor, resistor or cable. If you still want to do it like that, put a plastic washer between the nut and the circuit. Instead of the nuts, we recommend in this case to use a couple of our spacers (see spare parts in appendix)
22. If the circuit was without nuts, then put a couple of plastic washers to avoid the pressure to be exerted directly on the processor.

23. Now, if you want to install the serial connector, read on; if not go to step 11.
24. Pass the connector of the cable through port number one and in-between the battery-ports module.

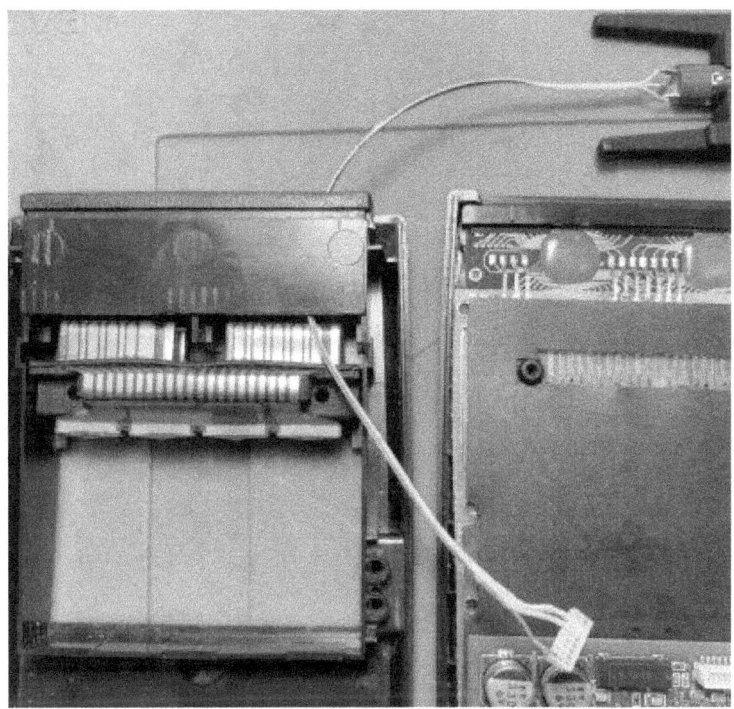

25. Secure with a piece of blu-tack the cable on the side. Make sure it goes really down because if not it will be caught when closing the calculator.

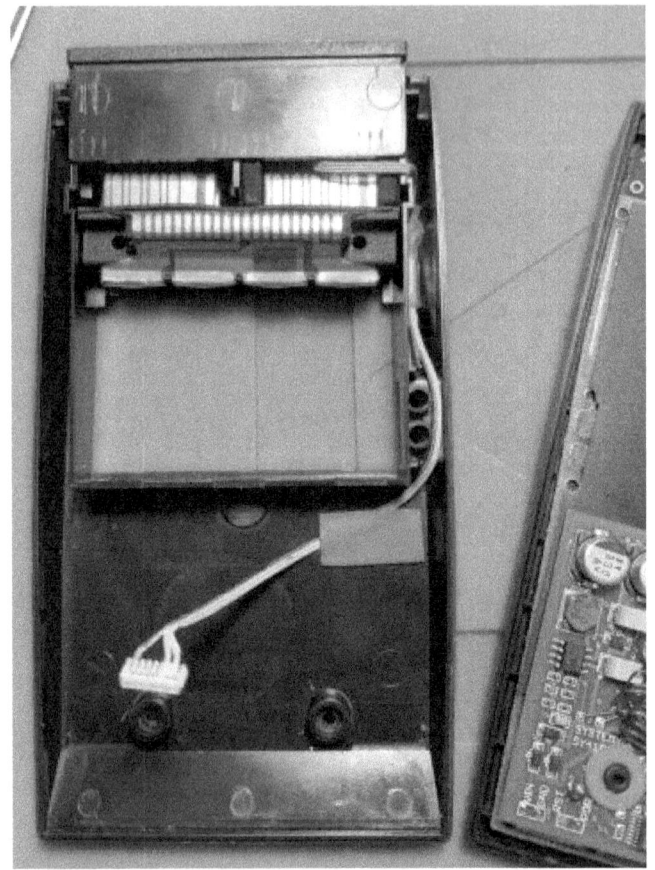

26. Insert the connector into the left female connector on the processor. Beware: it has only one correct way. Look at it with magnifier lenses.
27. Now, close the calculator following the instructions on chapter 5

Now, to initialize it, there are several ways to do it, explained in the Systemyde manual. My own procedure is the following:

First clear the memory management unit with the following command: XEQ Alpha MMUCLR Alpha

Then start loading necessary modules:

· Alpha YFNZ Alpha XEQ Alpha PLUG1L Alpha -

loading the YFNZ version of the utilities in the lower part of port 1

- Alpha PWRL Alpha XEQ Alpha PLUG1U Alpha - loading the PWRL version of the utilities in the upper part of port 1
- Alpha 804040–8120 Alpha XEQ Alpha YPOKE Alpha - loading the Library #4
- Finally, enable again the memory management unit: XEQ Alpha MMUEN Alpha.

Then, the system is ready to receive any ROM module, including those that use the Library#4 (Basically most of the modules created by Angel Martín) I then usually enter just the Advantage Pac and the latest version of Sandmath that I have in my CL - currently SM44, Sandmath4x4

16. PERIPHERAL REPAIRS AND OTHER ITEMS.

Some peripherals are quite impervious to damage (for example, the reading wand), but there are others that will develop faults every time. The most important of them is the card reader.

Hp 82104A Card Reader

All of them develop what has been called "gummy wheel disease": the rubber-like wheel that pushes the card through disintegrates into a sticky mess, which requires opening the machine, cleaning it thoroughly and putting another roller in its place.

From time to time we have also found other problems but the above one is 85% of all. Therefore, we will discuss first the gummy wheel repair and some troubleshooting.

You need to assume that every card reader that has not been repaired suffers from this problem. It will.

Parts required: one of:

- Teflon tubing. You can find it cut to length here in several eBay sellers – look in eBay for HP 41c card reader repair from user wnx72pt (no relation but a happy customer of him).
- Two silicon rubber rings – also from same source.

Better this one since the Teflon tubing has to be cut to length and it is difficult to do it straight.

In the case of the Teflon tubing, better to introduce the piece into the tube and cut from there to achieve a level cut.

Procedure:

1. Remove the label on the back of the card reader. Use a X-acto knife. Do it carefully because text may go together with it if not done with care.

2. Under the label there are three screws. Screw (1) is for opening the case. The two screws (2) hold the reader itself (the part with the motor) in place.

3. Remove the upper pair of screws on the side that faces the calculator back.

4. Pull up the body and remove the front plate. Pay
   attention to the two small pieces of metal sheet
   that work as springs. These are not glued and will
   fall apart. Put them aside; remember that the one
   covered with plastic is the one that sits beside the
   connectors between the case and the circuit. You will
   have to reassemble before closing the machine.

5. You now need to lift the circuit up. Be careful of not breaking the 4 springy pins that link the body to the circuit assembly. This part comes off after removing the screws (2) at the back of the reader.

6. You should leave all the wiring in place, but just in case one comes loose please remember the locations of all cables.

From top to bottom of the assembly:

- Red
- Yellow
- Blue
- Orange
- Black

The power cables that go to the electric motor are (from back to front, looking from the calculator side) Black and Red.

All these cables are very easy to disconnect: they are not soldered in place but pushed into a hole. Any tension will disconnect them. If that's the case, you will need to put them back in place with pliers.

Here you see the gummy wheel, held in place by the black pin shown.

The goo is extremely sticky – it will adhere to anything around.

7. To get to the wheel, you need to remove the motor. Unscrew the two screws that are quite difficult to reach and have a knack for falling to the ground.

8. Remove the plastic pin by pulling firmly but not too hard. It is the piece that hold the wheel in place. You can remove now the gummy wheel. It will have left residues in the cavity, that need to be removed with cotton swabs with alcohol.

9. Underneath the gummy wheel is a very small plastic roller. Make sure you do not lose it. It is very small and difficult to handle and has a tendency to fall to the floor and get lost. You need to clean it, anyway.

10. Now you need to clean with a X-acto knife, and finish it with alcohol until clean:

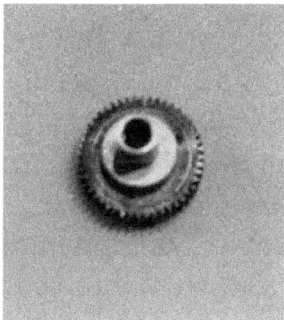

11. Now you need to put the two silicon rubber rings that you bought previously in eBay: (or the Teflon tubing on one side and cut from the other side)

12. Put the white plastic roller back in place. Again, avoid dropping it!

13. Put the refurbished wheel back in place, and put the pin but not introduce it yet.

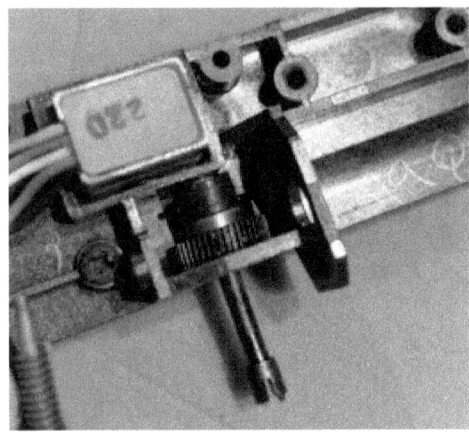

14. Reattach the motor with its screws. It helps to have a magnetic screwdriver. Do not tighten fully to make sure the alignment is right – once you check it, then you can tighten both screws.

15. Now you can put the pin fully into the hole.

16. Put the motor unit onto the back-plate. Make sure the five golden pins are in the holes and have contact.

17. Re-screw the screws:

18. You can safely test whether the card reader works without reassembling further.

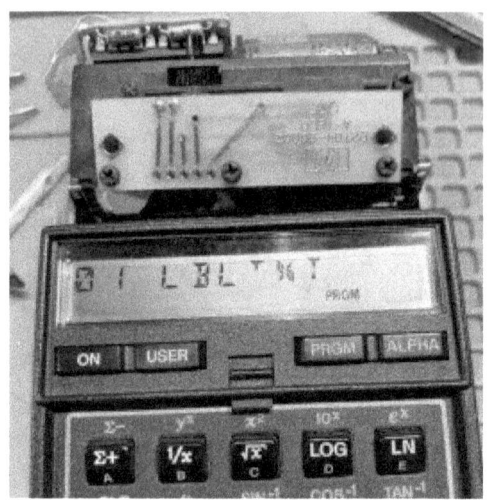

19. Now, pass a cleaner card (you may have it in the original card pack) several times through the hole. You need to have new batteries, since the card reader consumes a lot. The movement of the engine should be continuous and the sound regular. If it doesn't work, I bet that one of the cables in the reader is disconnected. If that is not the case, then this is a much more difficult case and the repair will probably not make economic sense – better to buy a new unit.

20. Usually I test it with a calculator without programs. I then write the "%T" program:

01 LBL "%T"
02 1/x
03 %
04 1/x
05 END

21. Then, in PRGM mode, you pass a card. It should show RDY CARD 1 of 1. It should be recorded on card now.

22. We delete the program (CLP) and make sure there is nothing in the program mode.

23. We exit PRGM mode. It should show 0.0000.

24. We pass the card again, now to read the program just written. It should show "WORKING" for a short while. If it shows "malfunction", check all connections again. If it shows "CARD ERROR", it may be the card, or you may need to clean the reading head. Do it and try again. If "WORKING", then check with CAT 1 if the program is again in memory. If so, you have your card reading working again!!

25. Time to reassemble the rest. It is a little bit involved, since the two springs need to be put with care to avoid being disassembled. First put them in place. The one covered in plastic is on the left:

26. Now put the front piece. You will need to hold it by hand when putting the top cover:

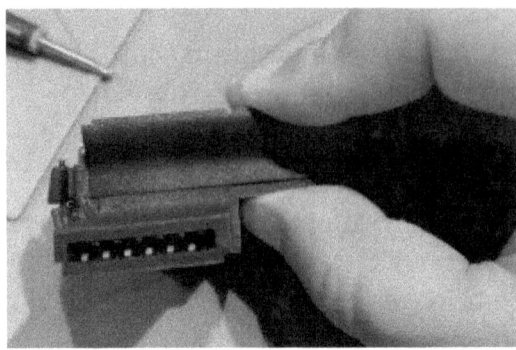

27. The pins with the holes for the small front screws need to fit into the top of the card reader case. Help it with pliers if it doesn't come in at first. Make sure that the left and right latches are as shown and both upper and lower pins fit in the holes of the lower and upper covers.

28. Now, put the top piece, making sure that:

   ◦ The pins with the holes for the front small screws fit into the top case
   ◦ The latches top and lower pins fit in their holes, and that they are straight enough so that the small tab in the back is *inside* the case.
   ◦ The front plate's top part fits inside the top half case

29. Once the top piece fits completely, screw in the front small screws and the lower screw (the longer of them all)

30. Now, re-attach the label. Normally it should keep enough glue to attach itself without any additional glue. You have finished! Test it again since there are some chances of disconnecting one of the cables when assembling the covers back – refer to step 18.

Motor Clutch issues

Once you have repaired the gummy wheel, you may find that the motor slips and you get a "MALFUNCTION" message. This is due to the electric motor "clutch" slipping. The noise is also quite ugly when that happens.
You need to follow the previous procedure from step 1 to step 7 included.

photo disassembled motor

Once disassembled the motor, you need to pull the screw part from the motor body with your fingers, not exerting too much force. Whe both parts are separated, you need to remove the matter inside the round cylinder with a needle. Do it gently: the cylinder walls are very thin and it is very easy to deform. Part of this matter may also be on the motor engine. Now we need to join again the motor, the endless screw and the cylinder together.

photo disassembled parts

Here I will show the procedure that I have been using. This procedure is NOT universally accepted. Many repairers think that the clutch should "give" a little, and be able to slip if the resistence is too big. Their solution is based on putting some small plastic tubing inside the cylinder, and put both endless screw and motor on either side by pressure.

photo cylinder with glue

The solution we propose is to fill the cylinder with E6000 glue, let it harden a little bit for 30 seconds, then introduce the endless screw and the motor in either side, remove the excess of glue with the tip of a needle or the point of a X-acto knife, mainly on the side of the motor axis (to avoid the motor to stop - this is critical), and let it dry in a position that ensures straigthness. Let it dry for 24 hours. Make sure that the axis moves freely from the motor, but does not move in relation with the endless screw.

With this repair, the assembly will have some compliance and tolerance to lack of straightness. We have found that the noise is lower and "nicer" when in operation.

Vinyl Case

A typical nuisance with old cases is that they generate black dust, that adheres to our calculators and darkens our screens. You need to blow the calculator every time to be able to use it! And you wonder if long exposure to that black dust will eventually damage the internal connections of the calculator.

In these cases, when you take the inner yellow sponge out of the case, it is black due to the dust.

The solution is very simple: wash the viny case by hand. First wash the sponge with soap (hand soap will do) until clean; then wash the case itself, applying generous droplets of soap and rubbing internally with your hands. Rinse thoroughly and wash it again. You will see that there is still dust falling out with the water drops, even after the second washing – though much less than the first time.

Let it dry overnight and problem solved!

For other problems with the vinyl case (zipper or unsewn parts), I'd take it to the local shoe repairer – here we can add no value.

Missing port covers

Many units sold over the internet had several memory or application modules that were removed for the sale (and sold separately to maximize value). Then, you get a calculator without one or more covers.

You can either find a new port cover in the auction sites (expensive when taking shipping into account) or buy new 3D printed units. However, these have a slightly different aspect, so we recommend buying the set of 4[xv]. You can then sell the rest of the ports you have and minimize the costs.

When all port covers are 3D, the aspect is good and consistent:

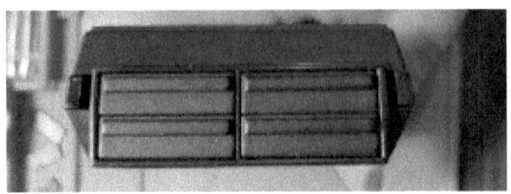

The side cover is more often present. The only reason to take it out was when there was an accumulator-battery module instead of normal batteries. However, when missing both options apply – find one in internet or buy a 3D printed unit[xvi]

Battery holder

We have already seen in chapter 5 that one of the possible failure reasons is corrosion on the springs of the battery module. I have seen several units that just required changing the springs to be brought back to life. Try first cleaning them with Caid-Deoxit. Alternatively (when corrosion is too extended) you can order springs from us[xvii]. These springs are done in 316 inox steel alloy.

When replacing the springs, make sure you clean thoroughly the case after taking the old ones out, so you have a nice, clean case. Caig Deoxit will do too.

The original battery holder has a couple of metal pieces that go between batteries, and that tend to get lost or heavily corroded over time. These are used to keep the batteries in place when the battery holder is taken out from the calculator. Otherwise, the spring effect will eject the batteries to the floor – been there many times!

Sometimes the battery holder itself is damaged. These are often seen in the auction sites, but due to price another alternative is a 3D printed piece like ours[xviii]. The one we have designed includes a nylon replica of the metal pieces that keep the batteries in place. The 3D piece is a little bit harder to plug in, in order to avoid it falling to the ground too often. You can see how it looks like within the machine:

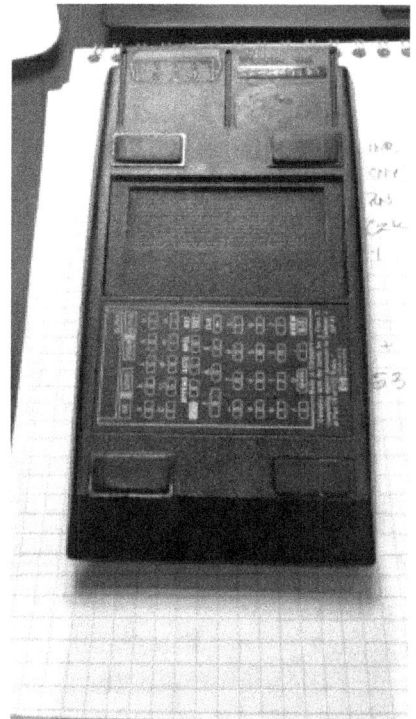

17. CLEANING AND MAINTENANCE

We receive many calculators each year, and many of them come in very dirty. In some cases they are so dirty that keyboard performance is affected.

Before anything else: **DO NOT PERFORM any of these procedures on an early, METAL KEYBOARD SURFACE calculator**. It will dissolve the black paint and it will destroy your calculator appearance. We repeat the statement above due to the importance of this advice. DO NOT USE CLEANERS for a calculator like the one on the right:

The basic cleaning we do is with leans cleaner. We spray over the full keyboard and screen. Then, clean the screen with a lint-free paper. The aspect will change a lot and the plastic will seem much more transparent.

Use cotton swabs to clean the rest of the keyboard. Clean the tops and the sides of the keys. The lettering on the top of the keys is molded into the key, so do not worry about rubbing strongly. The blue lettering is different, though. Do not worry about the liquid entering below the keyboard surface: there is a membrane that prevents the liquid entering the circuit (provided it doesn't "rain" on it!)

Clean also the surface of the keyboard by rubbing with the cotton swabs. You will be surprised about how dirty the swabs come out, and how many you need to use! Do not hesitate to apply another round of lens cleaner if the surface becomes dry before you feel it is clean.

Clean also the port holes. Here you can use Deoxit, since there are electrical connections that will benefit from it.

If there is any writing on the back, it can be removed with alcohol or Deoxit – depending on the felt pen used. Use sparingly. It can be used also to remove stickers.

Do not forget the battery cavity. Here you can also use Caig Deoxit, and remove all the green start of corrosion from the battery contacts. Make sure you also clean with Deoxit the springs of the battery box, and remove all traces of corrosion.

Vinyl case inner dust is treated in the previous chapter. However, external cleaning can be done with WD-40 embedded in a cloth. This will remove all writings and dirt, and will give a "new" appearance to your calculator.

Batteries

Here also Amazon is your friend. You can find many brands and types of LR1 – type N batteries. Beware of A21 batteries: they have roughly the same size but 12v instead of 1.5. They will fry your circuit with 48v instead of 6v! We believe that most of the screen driver damage comes from using the wrong batteries.

You can find refurbished accumulator packs (forget the old ones – they won't hold a charge after all these years). However, my preferred solution is the rechargeable N-type batteries, that you can also find in Amazon. ODEC is a brand that comes to mind, but there are more. They also sell the matching charger, that can be connected to a USB charger with USB nano connection. The charger can also be used for AAA batteries, with a clever adjustment device.

18. CONCLUSION

Well, by now I hope your calculator is working again. You may find (as I did) that it was fun to do it! Maybe you would like to repair more units!

In case you did not succeed, please let us know and see how we can help you. In our experience, most units that are difficult to repair are due to screen problems – normally a defective screen driver. These are difficult to find – you'll need to find a donor. Try to find a defective unit in the usual auction sites – most likely the screen driver will be fine (even if the LCD is blackened)

Anyway, we'd like to know from you. You can as well give us feedback on the book, or if you missed something that you wanted covered in the book. You can email us to sales@thecalculatorstore.com, and let us know how it went.

AKNOWLEDGEMENTS

This book could not have been written without the support and encouragement of my wife, Olga, and the expertise and knowledge of Ignacio Sánchez, who developed many of the repair methods and procedures in this book. I am indebted to his knowledge and advice.

APPENDIX 1: THE CALCULATOR STORE SPARE PARTS

After our many repairs of HP41 calculators, we have learned many simple methods; many of them from contributors to hpmuseum.org; however, we have found a number of cases where the solutions available did not work, and we had to locate or design our own parts. Here is a list of them

Flex PCB

A design from Diego Díaz, is still valid to repair corroded battery contacts. However, while it will repair your unit now, our experience is that in many cases the adhesive will fail after some time – both on the front and the module adaptor.

Flex PCB assembled:

http://www.thecalculatorstore.com/Assembly-kit-for-HP-41c-battery-bay-and-expansion-ports

Taking Diego's design, we have developed a 3D base for the PCB, but we fix the modules' area and the front connectors with two additional pieces and screws, so that it is impossible that it becomes loose – on both extremes. This is our best seller and it is a direct drop-in part – no need to fuss about installation

Flex PCB assembled – flat:
http://www.thecalculatorstore.com/Assembled-HP-41c-battery-bay-and-expansion-ports-module-Flat

Same design as the previous one, but with a flat bottom. It is designed to be glued to a flat back half (when the screw supports are broken, and remains removed with a Dremel machine). It is effectively a brokenback + Flex PCB assembled together.

The risk is that, if it needs to be repaired again, it will be much more difficult.

Brokenback
http://www.thecalculatorstore.com/Piece-for-repair-of-back-case-of-HP41C

Designed to replace the screw supports in the upper part of the back side of the calculator. To be glued in place. The back side upper screw supports' remains need to be removed with a Dremel or similar.

Battery holder:
http://www.thecalculatorstore.com/Battery-holder-3D

Developed in 3D HP Multijet technology, it is a replacement for the often broken original battery holder. It has small springy sections to avoid the batteries jumping out when opening the batteries (same as in the original battery holder with the small metallic pieces). It has a couple of stainless steel springs (our design), which are the longest of the three lengths we have encountered in original battery holders.

Stainless steel springs
http://www.thecalculatorstore.com/HP41c-battery-holder-spring

We have designed a stainless spring couple that can be used in the HP41c original and 3D battery holders (two units required) and for the Woodstock calculators (HP21, HP22, HP25, etc. 1 required)

Port covers:
http://www.thecalculatorstore.com/HP41c-Port-cover-3D

There are many calculators that have lost one or several back covers over time: here a module, there a card reader…and then you want all 4 covers. You can try to find original covers in the usual sites, or you can buy our 3D replica. As it is not 100% equal to the originals, we sell it by fours, to make sure that when you replace all, it will look OK no matter what.

Side cover:
http://www.thecalculatorstore.com/HP41c-side-cover

Many units (in particular those that had accumulator module) have lost their side covers. We have created a 3D replica that is good enough for any calculator.

Lower post repair piece
http://www.thecalculatorstore.com/Lower-Post-Repair-par

Used when the lower posts (or one of them) are broken. The idea is to give enough adhesive area to avoid rotation when introducing the screws. To be used with E6000 glue.

Upper post repair piece
http://www.thecalculatorstore.com/Upper-Post-Repair-part

Same for the upper posts. To be used with E6000 glue.

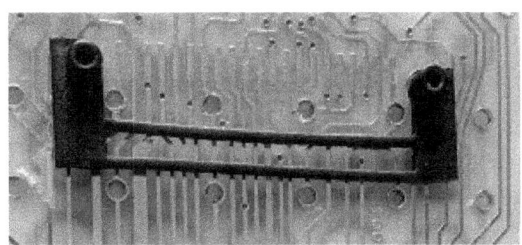

Zebra for full-nut units

http://www.thecalculatorstore.com/Zebra-connector-for-HP41C-repair

Made off a folded-down flexible PCB, a direct replacement of part no. 1251-5731. It has an elastomer round core, and the spacing is equal to that of the connectors of both the processor and keyboard circuit.

Spacers

http://www.thecalculatorstore.com/Space-set-for-repairing-old-HP41c/en

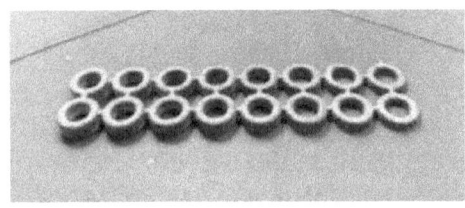

This is a substitute for the original nuts that can be seen in early HP41 full-nuts. In these, the processor circuit was pressed to the keyboard circuit by screwing a couple of nuts on the screw posts.

Our experience is that these posts will not withstand many screwing and unscrewing before breaking. And it is difficult to screw them just enough to have an even pressure on the zebra connector. You will need to try – and we've broken many a post when reassembling.

The newer calculators used the pressure from the back side of the calculator on the processor. We use the same principle with these spacers. We have printed a set with different heights, in 0.2mm increments, so that you can adapt to different processor circuit thicknesses. In addition, the inner diameter is quite tight, so it can also help to keep so-so screw posts together (using also the procedure with superglue explained in chapter 10)

Screws:
http://www.thecalculatorstore.com/lower-post-long-screw-inox (can also be found in black for purists)

Upper screws are seldom broken but sometimes lost. The lower screws we sell are slightly longer than the original, and equal to the ones used by HP service when repairing calculators. Sometimes the screw post thread is not working anymore, and you just need a couple of additional millimeters of thread to be able to close the calculator – without additional repair efforts. You can have them in black as well.

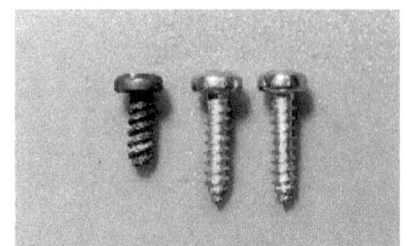

APPENDIX 2:HP41C
LIST OF PARTS

Table 6-1. HP-41 Replaceable Parts

INDEX NUMBER, FIGURE 6-1	HP PART NUMBER	DESCRIPTION	QTY
1	00041-60009	ASSEMBLY, battery case (A5)	1
	00041-40005	o CASE, battery	1
	00041-20003	o KEEPER, battery	2
	1460-3695	o SPRING, battery	2
2*	00041-60512	ASSEMBLY, display (A2)	1
	00041-60140	o ASSEMBLY, display driver (A2U2)	1
	1600-1850	o CLIP, display	2
	1251-7987	o CONNECTOR, display (A2P1)	2
	1990-0798	o DISPLAY, liquid crystal (LCD)	1
	0340-0919	o INSULATOR, display	2
	00041-40147	o LOCATOR, display	1
	0460-1553	o TAPE, adhesive transfer	
3	00041-60XXX	ASSEMBLY, logic PC (A3)	1
4	00041-60008	ASSEMBLY, I/C (A4)	1
5	00041-60307	ASSEMBLY, keyboard, service (A1)	1
	7121-0332	OVERLAY, (41C)	1
	7121-1334	OVERLAY, (41CV/CX)	1
6**	00041-20002	BALL, ac contact	2
7	00041-60100	CASE, bottom	1
8	00041-40006	CASE, center	1
9	1251-5731	CONNECTOR, logic (P2)	1
10	00041-40026	COVER, ac tunnel	1
11	4040-1522	COVER, battery recess	1
12	00041-40007	DOOR, I/O blank	4
13	0403-0279	FOOT, rubber	4
14	7120-8153	LABEL, logo (41C)	1
	7121-1848	LABEL, logo (41CV)	1
	00041-80021	LABEL, logo (41CX)	1
15	7120-8154	LABEL, alpha (41C/CV)	1
	00041-80022	LABEL, alpha (41CX)	1
16	3050-1051	SPACER, 0.80-inch (white)	2
	3050-1111	SPACER, 0.75-inch (red)	2
	3050-1112	SPACER, 0.70-inch (blue)	2
	2740-0014	NUT, hex	2
	2740-0013	NUT, hex (undersized)	2
17**	00041-40067	RETAINER, ac contact	1
18	0624-0435	SCREW, 0.25-inch	2
	0624-0436	SCREW, 0.36-inch (oversized)	
19	0624-0432	SCREW, 0.75-inch	2
20	00041-40064	SHIELD, display	1
21**	1460-1767	SPRING, ac contact	2
22***	00041-20005	WASHER, 0.013 inch	4

* When updating from a rev F display driver hybrid (square plastic cover over IC's) you must replace C2 with a 470uf capacitor.
** Removed on later versions.
*** Use only with the 5081-5564 logic board.

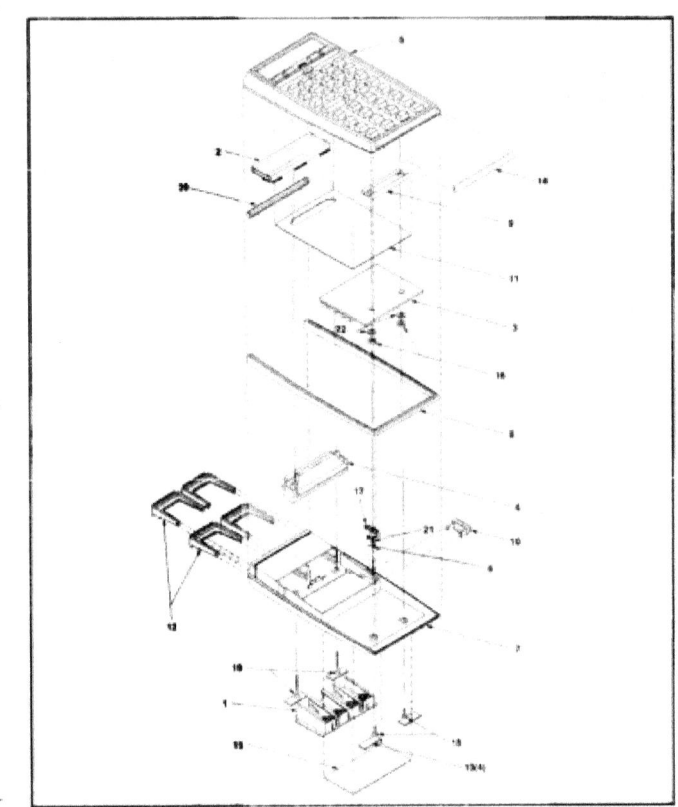

Figure 6-1. HP-41 Exploded View

118

APPENDIX 3: FULL-NUT CIRCUITS

Shown here just to identify vintage and type (C, CV or CX). Value changes dramatically from one to the other!

Early C model (not the first design). Always seen secured with nuts. Called "two transistors" in Service manual

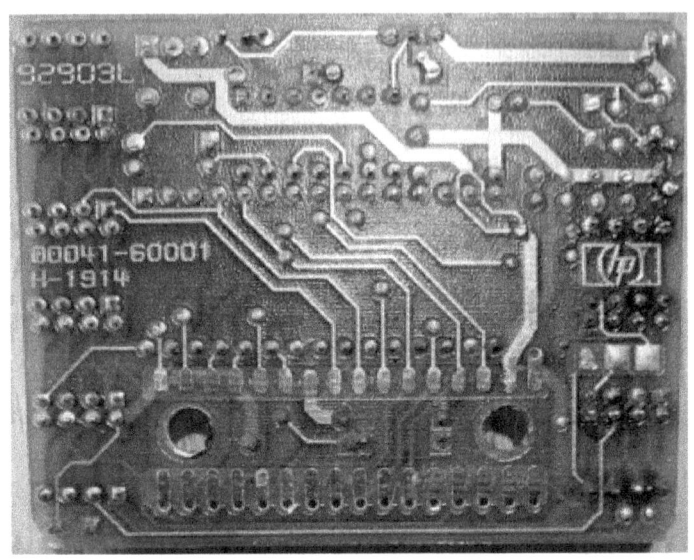

C-model: Final circuit

Newer C model. This model boardwas compatible with CV – just adding more memory. Codes for C were always 60105 (with the "4" painted over)

C model: newer circuit. Common board for C, CV and CX. This was printed in a different support, thinner, which required washers to ensure good connection. Two last codes (CV and CXP) painted over.

CV model. Observe is the same circuit of the second C, but showing 60104 instead

CX model. Note the dark green circuit. It is thinner and requires spacers to provide good pressure and thus connection to main circuit. Observe is the common board for C, CV and CX, with the two first code numbers painted over.

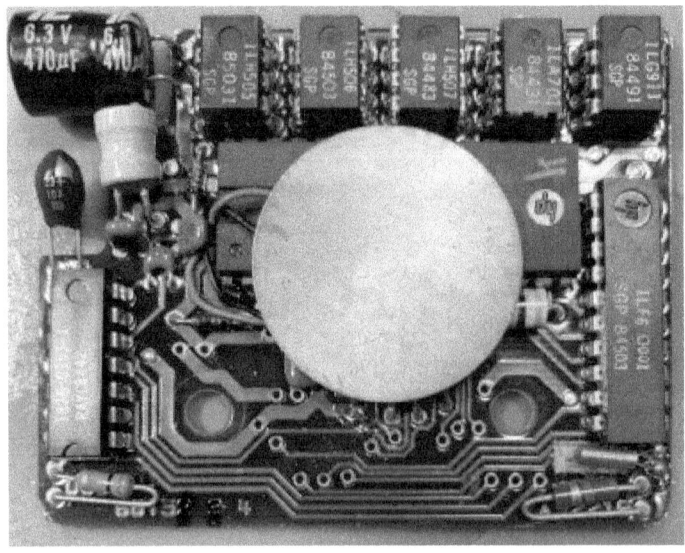

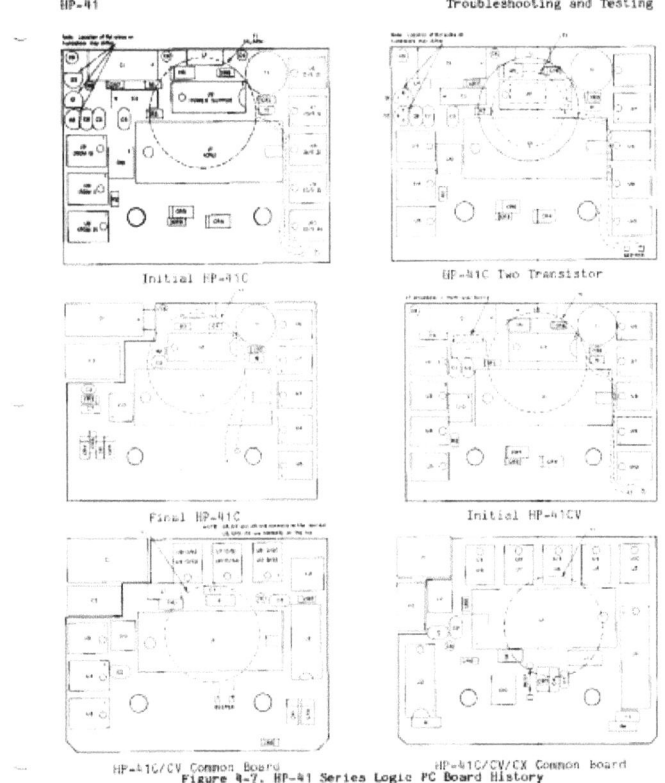

Initial HP-41C   HP-41C Two Transistor

Final HP-41C   Initial HP-41CV

HP-41C/CV Common Board   HP-41C/CV/CX Common Board

Figure 4-7. HP-41 Series Logic PC Board History

4-35/4-36

125

APPENDIX 4: LIST OF SOFTWARE MODULES

This is the list and size of the modules currently integrated in the CL module. It is shown as reference in order to find the software you may need.

The first field is the ROM file name, that can be found in HP41.org (together with the manuals and other information); the second is the code used in HP41CL (you need to enter the name in the Alpha register and then execute PLUGx, being X the virtual port you want to use); the third is the module ID number (you can't have two modules plugged in with the sam ID number), and the fourth is a short description of what the module does. More information can be found in hp41.org.

Contents	ID	XROM	Description
NUT0-N.ROM	OS41	N/A	HP Operating System Rev N
XFNS3-3B.ROM	XFN3	25	HP CX Extended Functions 3B
SERVICE.ROM	HSRV	N/A	HP Service 2A
XFNS5-2D.ROM	XFN5	N/A	HP CX Extended Functions 2D
TIME-3A.ROM	TMOD	26	HP CX Time Functions 3A
YFNZ-4F.ROM	YFNZ	15	41CL Extra Functions -4F
ADVL1-1B.ROM	41AD	22	HP-41 Advantage Pac 1B
YFNX-4C.ROM	YFNX	15	41CL Extreme Functions -4C
YLIB-5A.ROM	YLIB	N/A	41CL Library Functions -5A
ADVU1-1B.ROM	41AD	24	HP-41 Advantage Pac 1B
MPL2V1F.ROM	MLTI	3	Multiprecision Library ROM
YFNP-1F.ROM	YFNP	15	41CL Extra Functions Plus -1F
AECROML.ROM	AECR	18	AECROM

AUTOFIN.ROM	AFIN	21	GMAC Autofinance
ASSEM3.ROM	ASMB	21	Assembler 3
AUTOSTRT.ROM	AUTO	10	HP Autostart
AVIATION.ROM	AVIA	19	HP Aviation Pac 1A
HELPSYS.ROM	HELP	10	Help System
GAMEZONE.ROM	ZONE	10	Game Zone
CCDL-1B.ROM	CCDR	9	CCD Module 1B
CHEMUSER.ROM	CHEM	20	Chemistry Solutions book
CIRCUIT.ROM	CIRC	6	HP Circuit Analysis Pac 1A
CLINICAL.ROM	CLIN	19	HP Clinical Lab & Nuclear Medicine Pac 1A
DATAACQL.ROM	DACQ	21	HP Data Acquisition 1B
DAVID-2C.ROM	DAVA	2	David Assembler 2C
HPILDEVL.ROM	DEVI	22	HP HP-IL Development Pac 1B
HPILDIAG.ROM	DIIL	19	HP HP- IL Diagnostic
DIAMOND.ROM	DMND	31	Diamond
ES41L.ROM	E41S	4	ES41
ESMLDL.ROM	ESML	10	ESMLDL 7B
EXTIO-1A.ROM	EXIO	23	HP Extended I/O 1A
FINANCE.ROM	FINA	4	HP Financial Decisions Pac 1D
GAMES-1A.ROM	GAME	10	HP Games Pac 1A
GMAC2.ROM	GMAS	31	GMAC 2
GMAC3L.ROM	GMAT	21	GMAC 3
HEPX1-1E.ROM	HEPX	7	HEPAX 1D, bnk 1
HOMEMGT.ROM	HOME	9	HP Home Management Pac 1A
LABELS.ROM	LBLS		LABELS
LANDNAV.ROM	LAND	1	LANDNAV
MATH-1D.ROM	MATH	1	HP Math Pac 1D
MACHINE.ROM	MCHN	12	HP Machine Design Pac 1A
MELBRNE.ROM	MELB	12	Melbourne
MIL-ENGL.ROM	MILE	21	Military Engineering
MLROM.ROM	MLRM	21	MLROM
NAVL-1B.ROM	NAVI	14	HP Navigation Pac 1B
NFCROM.ROM	NFCR	17	NFCROM 1B
NAVCOM2L.ROM	NVCM	14	NAVCOM 2
PCODER.ROM	PCOD	16	ProtoCoder 1A

BOOST1.ROM	BSTZ	6	Boost, bnk 1
SW_DEVL.ROM	SWSW	6	Software Development German book
PRAXIS.ROM	VIEW	9	Programs from Vieweg book
PETROLL.ROM	PETR	15	HP Petroleum Fluids Pac 1A
PLOTTERL.ROM	PLOT	17	HP Plotter Pac 1A
PPCL.ROM	PPCM	10	PPC ROM pg 1
REALESTL.ROM	REAL	11	HP Real Estate Pac 1A
QUATERL.ROM	QUAT	15	Quaternion
SECURITY.ROM	SECY	19	HP Securities Pac 1A
STANDARD.ROM	STAN	5	HP Standard Applications Pac 1C
SGS-GAS.ROM	SGSG	21	SGS GAS
SIM12L.ROM	SIMM	4	Surveyor Inc. Module pg 1
SKWIDBC.ROM	SKWD	8	SKWID
SIMPLEX.ROM	SMPL	16	Simplex
STAT-1B.ROM	STAT	2	HP Statistics Pac 1B
STRESS.ROM	STRE	8	HP Stress Analysis Pac 1A
STRUCTL.ROM	STRU	7	HP Structural Analysis Pac 1B
SUPRROML.ROM	SUPR	21	SUP-R-ROM
SURVEY.ROM	SURV	3	HP Survey Pac 1B
THERMAL.ROM	THER	13	HP Thermal & Transport Science Pac 1A
DISASM4C.ROM	DA4C	15	DisAsm 4C
PPCSTAT1.ROM	PPC9	9	PPC Statistics
UPDAT-4D.ROM	YUPS	31	41CL Update Functions -4D
UPHST-2A.ROM	YCLN	31	41CL Clone Functions -2A
CLILUP.ROM	YUIL	14	41CL IL Update Functions
YREGAPPS.ROM	YRGA	21	YREG Applications
HANDY.ROM	HNDY	31	Handy Compact
ASTRO-1.ROM	ASTT	6	Astro-2010
CHESS1.ROM	CHES	8	Chess
FUN1.ROM	FUNS	10	Funstuff
JMBMATHL.ROM	JMAT	5	JMB-Math
SLANTR.ROM	SR1B	11	SLANTR-SR1B
QUEENS.ROM	QUEN	9	N-Queens
KRAUSS1.ROM	KRSS	17	Krauss book

TREKKIES.ROM	TREK	11	Trekkies
UNITCONV.ROM	UNIT	10	UNITCONV
BMF1.ROM	ADV1	12	Adventure
BMF5.ROM	ADV2	13	Adventure
CFIT1.ROM	CURV	4	CurveFit
MATRIX1.ROM	JMTX	8	JMB-Matrix
DISASM4D.ROM	DASM	15	DisAsm 4D
EXT-IL.ROM	EXTI	27	SKWID EXT-IL
CCD-OSX.ROM	CCDX	5	CCD-OSX
SANDBOXL.ROM	SBOX	8	Sandbox
PANAMEL.ROM	PANA	5	Paname
83TRINH.ROM	TRIH	9	83trinh
ADV-APP.ROM	AADV	19	Advantage Applications
OS4.ROM	4OS4	N/A	OS Page 4 Extension, bnk 1
LADYBUG1.ROM	LADY	16	Ladybug, bnk 1
AMCOSX4.ROM	AOSX	5	LIBRARY-4 AMC-OSX
ASSEMB4.ROM	ASM4	21	Assembler 4
ASTROLGY.ROM	ALGY	31	ASTRO-ROM
AV1.ROM	AV1Q	31	AV1
BCMW.ROM	BCMW	8	BCMW
CVPAK1.ROM	CVPK	21	CVPAK
DYERKA.ROM	DYRK	31	Dyerka
FORTH4.ROM	FRTH	N/A	HP-41 FORTH
HYDRACMP.ROM	COMP	21	Hydracomp
ICODE.ROM	ICOD	19	Icode
LAITRAM.ROM	LAIT	N/A	Laitram-XQ2
MCTEST.ROM	MTST	3	Mctest
MDP1L.ROM	MDP1	15	MDP1
MDP2L.ROM	MDP2	17	MDP2
MUECKEL.ROM	MUEC	21	Muecke
NAVPAC2L.ROM	NPAC	14	Navpac
OILWELLL.ROM	OILW	21	Oilwell
PARIO.ROM	PARI	14	ProtoPario
PS0F.ROM	PS0F	16	ProfiSet -0F
PPC-MELB.ROM	PMLB	12	PPC-Melbourne
PRIDE1.ROM	PRIQ	21	Pride

ROAM-0A.ROM	ROAM 5	ROAM
ROMSV01.ROM	ROMS 9	Romsv01
PRISMFUN.ROM	FUNP 10	PRISMA Fun
SPEED2L.ROM	SMCH 21	Speed Machine II
TOMSROM.ROM	TOMS 6	Tomsrom
ZENROM.ROM	ZENR 5	Zenrom
ZEPROM.ROM	ZEPM 9	Zeprom
EVAL_3K.ROM	FRML 30	Formula Evaluation
EVAL_APP.ROM	FRMX 31	Formula Evaluation Applications
HEPRAM.ROM	HEPR N/A	HEPAX RAM Template
NYCS1.ROM	NYSB 30	New York City Subway Map
SPECTRAL.ROM	SPEC 8	Spectral Analysis
KNIGHTTR.ROM	KNGT 31	JMB Knightís Tour
MARKS3A.ROM	DBUG 3	(RAM only) HP-41 MCODE Debugger
MLABELS.ROM	MLBL N/A	Mainframe Labels
BESSEL1.ROM	BESL 2	Bessel Functions
POLYN1.ROM	POLY 6	Polynomial Functions
ILBUFFER.ROM	ILBF 22	IL Buffer
NOVCHAP.ROM	NCHP 31	NOV CHAP
MPATHS.ROM	METX 30	MetroX
MMADRID.ROM	5MAD N/A	Madrid, Spain Metro Map (for METX)
DIFFGEOM.ROM	GEOD 31	Differential Geometry
ISENE.ROM	ISEN 17	ISENE
BSMS.ROM	BSMS 18	Bus. Sales/Marketing/Stats Solution Book
CNTLSYS.ROM	CNTL 14	Control Systems Solution Book
ELECENG.ROM	EENG 15	Electrical Engineering Solution Book
LENDLS.ROM	LNDL 19	Lend/Lease Savings Solution Book
TESTSTAT.ROM	TEST 13	Test Statistics Solution Book
MECHENG.ROM	MENG 16	Mechanical Engineering Solution Book
XROM.ROM	ROMX 31	XROM
ANTENNAS.ROM	ANTS 16	Antennas Solution Book
OPTOMTR.ROM	OPTO 16	Optometry Solution Book

PHYSICS.ROM	PHYH	15	Physics Solution Book
GEOMETRY.ROM	GEOM	14	Geometry Solution Book
HL_MATH.ROM	HMAT	12	High-Level Math Solution Book
INTSOLN.ROM	ISOL	11	Interchangeable Solutions UPLE Program
TIMERSLN.ROM	TIME	6	Timer Solution Book
GRAFIKS1.ROM	GRF1	9	Grafiks
GRAFIKS3.ROM	GRF3	10	Grafiks
CAB41L.ROM	CAB4	21	Schenk CAB 41
FLDB.ROM	FLDB	N/A	41CL Flash YCRC Database
IMDB.ROM	IMDB	N/A	41CL Image Database
GASPRP1.ROM	GASL	1	GASPROP
GPROPP5.ROM	GASU	5	GASPROP
AEC3L.ROM	AEC3	18	AECROM III pg 1
BLDROM.ROM	BLDR	17	Build ROM
UPLMTH1.ROM	UPLM	13	Userís Program Library - Math, page 1
BGUG_IDC.ROM	IDC1	21	Blood Glucose UG
ML-IDC_L.ROM	IDC2	21	ML-Insulin Dosage Computer
REGULA1.ROM	REGU	9	Control Systems
GEIR.ROM	ISEM	23	Geir
MLONDON.ROM	5LON	N/A	London, England Tube Map (for METX)
PROFIL.ROM	PRFS	27	Profiset
VIEIRA.ROM	LUIZ	17	Luiz Vieiraís Collection
MAZES.ROM	MAZZ	16	Mazes and Puzzle Games
MAHJONG1.ROM	MAHJ	10	Mahjong
IERF1.ROM	IERR	1	IERF
ACTION1.ROM	AGAM	13	Action Games
ADVPRT1.ROM	ADVP	11	Advanced Printer
SWAP21.ROM	2SWP	10	Misc routines from 412 Swap Disks
CCDADV.ROM	CCDA	10	CCD Advanced
GEOMTRY.ROM	GMTY	16	Geometry 11
PASCAL41.ROM	APSC	20	PASCAL & Data Banks
NUMTHRY.ROM	NTHY	16	Number Theory
DIGITPAC.ROM	DIGT	24	DigitPAC

ILDEV2L.ROM	DEV2	22	IL Development II
MONOPLY1.ROM	MONO	16	MONOPOLY
RAMBOX32.ROM	RM32	31	RAMBox32
EPIDEMIC.ROM	EPIV	31	Epidemics
SUDOKU.ROM	SUD1	16	SUDOKU
VECTORS.ROM	VECT	14	Vector Analysis
HDISASM.ROM	HDIS	9	HEPAX Disassembler
YACHTL.ROM	YACH	21	Bobby Schenkís Yacht
EXILPS.ROM	EILP	27	Extended IL Plus
CLUTLSB1.ROM	PWRL	12	Power-CL Utilities, bnk 1
DIFEQ1.ROM	DIFF	15	Differential Equations
INTEG1.ROM	INTG	16	Integrator
SIROM.ROM	SIHP	27	Solve & Integrate
PRTSRVC.ROM	PSRV	N/A	Printer Service
EVAL_EQN.ROM	SLVF	31	Formula Evaluation Equations
GELENKGT.ROM	GLNG	16	Gelengegetribe Konstruktion
LIBRARY4.ROM	4LIB	N/A	Library-4
RAMPGX4.ROM	4RAM	17	Library-4 RAMpage X
TBOX4_L4.ROM	4TBX	13	Library-4 Toolbox
ALPHA44.ROM	4ALP	6	Library-4 Alpha
HP67_FUN.ROM	H67G	23	HP-67 Games
OUTERPLN.ROM	OPLN	21	Outer Planets
RAWGM1.ROM	RGME	18	RAW Games
SYSDEMO1.ROM	DEMO	14	HP41 System Demo
XMASSTG.ROM	MASS	16	Extended Mass Storage
41ZDIAG.ROM	4DIG	8	Library-4 41Z Diagnostic
N-BODY.ROM	NBOD	6	Gravitational N-Body Problems
CHEMENG.ROM	CENG	12	Chemical Engineering Solutions
SNEAP1.ROM	NEA1	21	SNEAP
SNEAP3.ROM	NEA3	11	SNEAP
SNEAP5.ROM	NEA5	13	SNEAP
KERMI2K.ROM	KRMK	1	Kermit 2000
FLUIDDYN.ROM	FDYN	17	Fluid Dynamics Solutions
SWPGAME1.ROM	GSWP	9	Swap Games
HVAC.ROM	HVAC	16	HVAC Solutions
SOLARENG.ROM	LENG	14	Solar Engineering Solutions

SAMLUNG1.ROM	GRMK	10	Games from Sammlung book
FAIRFLDL.ROM	FAIR	21	Fairfield
LAPLACE1.ROM	LPLC	10	Laplace Transform
RSU_OSL.ROM	ROSV	4	RSU OS
HEPX4H_1.ROM	HEP2	7	HEPAX 4H, bnk 1
BASIC1.ROM	BASI	8	BASIC
CMT-300L.ROM	CMT3	9	CMT-300 Multimeter
XPLORE1.ROM	GAMX	12	Explore Games
CMT-200.ROM	CMT2	4	CMT-200 Data Acquisition
MLEPR_1H.ROM	EPRH	4	MLEPR -1H
BUDER2L.ROM	BUD2	15	Buderus-2
BUDER3.ROM	BUD3	9	Buderus-
MWKLN3.ROM	MWK3	10	MWK-3
MWKLN4L.ROM	MWK4	21	MWK-4
OVTROP2L.ROM	OTRP	5	Oventrop Ventil
NEXT_2C.ROM	NEXT	6	NEXT
MOUNT1C.ROM	MCMP	15	Mountain Computer 1C
CMT_1.ROM	CMT1	31	CMT-100 Eprom Test
ICEBOX1H.ROM	IBOX	4	ICEbox -1H
MMEPROM.ROM	EPRM	16	MMEPROM
SRVC-1D.ROM	YSV1	N/A	41CL-specific HP Service (41C version)
SRVC-2B.ROM	YSV2	N/A	41CL-specific HP Service (CV/CX version)
ADVTGMTH.ROM	ADVG	12	Advantage Math
NONLINR.ROM	NONL	17	Non-linear Systems Module
4WINS.ROM	4WIN	16	Connect Four Game
PSRVC-2C.ROM	YSV3	N/A	41CL-specific HP Printer Service
ELIPAPPS.ROM	ELIX	16	Orbital Mechanics
YFNF-3A.ROM	YFNF	16	41CL Memory Functions -3A
OSXB1.ROM	OSX3	5	Lib-4 OS/X Bank-Switched, bnk 1
WWRAMBOX.ROM	WRAM	31	W&W Rambox64
OBCSYS.ROM	OBCZ	31	OBCSYS
AECPROG.ROM	PROG	18	Program Generator
AECSLVR.ROM	GSLV	18	Geometric Solver
BBS1.ROM	BBSC	11	Bank Beratungs Software

DST12_1L.ROM	DST1	8	CalTrans Survey
U-BAHN.ROM	5UBH	N/A	Berlin, Germany U-Bahn Map (for METX)
MATPOL11.ROM	4MTI	22	Lib-4 Matrix/Polynomial
ETSII4A.ROM	ETS4	8	ETSII4A
MATPOL21.ROM	4MTI	24	Lib-4 Matrix/Polynomial
ETSII5A.ROM	ETS5	10	ETSII5A
PWREXT1.ROM	PWRX	12	PowerCL Extreme, bnk 1
VERMPACK.ROM	VERM	27	Vermpack 1A
TVM_1E.ROM	TVMY	22	TVM 1E
NUTIP-1A.ROM	ITCP	4	NutIP TCP/IP 1A
SIMPLEX2.ROM	LPLX	8	Linear Programming
FORCAST1.ROM	FCST	10	Market Forecaster -1
FORCAST2.ROM	FCS2	10	Market Forecaster -2
SUNSHT-1.ROM	COOQ	31	Sunshot
SSHEET.ROM	SHTZ	8	Spreadsheet
INDOOR.ROM	INDO	10	Philips Indoor Lighting
ETSII3A.ROM	ETS3	12	ETSII3A
FCALAS1.ROM	FSSY	14	FOCAL Assmbly/Disassembly
FOR_FEE.ROM	FFEE	14	For Fee
ETSII6A.ROM	ETS9	16	ETSII6A
CVLENG.ROM	CIVI	16	HP Civil Engineering Solutions
CIVU1.ROM	CIVU	20	Civil Engineering Special Collection
CRTVONK.ROM	VONK	16	Math Programs Collection
CLXPREGS.ROM	XPMM	20	CL Expanded Memory Functions
CCDAPPS.ROM	UCCD	18	CCD Manual examples
ANGEL-1.ROM	ANGZ	3	Angel ZEPROM
TMAX3A.ROM	TMAX	6	Turbo-MAX 3A
BJ1B.ROM	BLJK	7	Blackjack -1B
MAX2E.ROM	BJMX	6	Blackjack MAX -2E
VEGAS1C.ROM	VEGS	6	Vegas -1C
SMAT41.ROM	SM44	3	Lib-4 Sandmath 4x4
PPCAPPS1.ROM	PPCU	17	PPC User Applications
WWDAPPS.ROM	WWDB	17	Wickes, Wlodek, Dearing books
JARRETXF.ROM	JARR	17	K. Jarrett XF book

RAWFL_1.ROM	GRAW	18	Geneís RAW files
MCCRNAK.ROM	MCCK	16	Alan McCornack book
GERMAN1.ROM	KRGM	17	Kruse/Gosmann books
PK_ALPH.ROM	PKP1	31	Poul Kaarupís Alpha and Pointers
PK_MATH.ROM	PKP2	14	Poul Kaarupís Math and Physics
PK_FLAG.ROM	PKP3	3	Poul Kaarupís Flags and Stack
PK_PROG.ROM	PKP4	5	Poul Kaarupís Program Utilities
PK_TIME.ROM	PKP5	18	Poul Kaarupís Timer and Utilities
WARPB1.ROM	WARP	21	Warp-core, bnk 1
TEXTED.ROM	EDTR	8	Text Editor
HP-16C_1.ROM	16CS	16	HP-16C Emulator -1A, bnk 1
HC_1.ROM	HCPL	10	Hyper-Complex Math
MPARIS.ROM	5PAR	N/A	Paris, France Metro Map (for METX)
PSYCHRO.ROM	STEQ	12	Steam Properties
POKER.ROM	PPOK	10	Poker and Blackjack
GRAVTIM1.ROM	GRVI	16	Gravity & Time
NUT0-HT.ROM	HT41	N/A	H. Thorngrenís modified OS
TIME-HT.ROM	HTP5	26	H. Thorngrenís modified OS
NASA.ROM	NASA	16	Flight and Aeronautics Papers
HOROSCOP.ROM	HORO	16	Horoscope
TIDES.ROM	TIDW	10	Tides
PORTSL.ROM	PRTW	11	US Ports
HPCALEND.ROM	CLND	12	HP Calendar Solutions
RUBIKS.ROM	RUBK	8	Rubikís Cube
HEATEX.ROM	BBDY	16	Heat Exchange
CPXMTRX.ROM	ZMAT	13	Complex Matrices
JMB_CAL.ROM	JMBC	17	JMB Calendar
USERCAL.ROM	UCLN	18	User Calendar
FILTERS1.ROM	EEFD	17	EE Filter Design
CRYPTO41.ROM	CRTO	10	Cryptography
XFRAME.ROM	XBFR	30	Direct Stiffness Method
TRUSS.ROM	XTRS	30	Direct Stiffness Method: Trusses
SWAPMTH.ROM	3SWP	12	Swapdisk Math
XMSTAT.ROM	XTAT	6	XM Statistics Module
TRANSNEP.ROM	EPTN	23	Trans-Neptunian Planets, 2016-2025

COUNTRY.ROM	CITY	30	Country/Capital
SERIES.ROM	SERI	18	Sums & Series
PLANETS.ROM	PLAN	9	Planets
PLUTOIDS.ROM	PLTO	10	Plutoids
SPANISH.ROM	WORD	31	English/Spanish Dictionary
GJM_2B_1.ROM	GJMR	31	Greg J McClureís
ELLIPTIC.ROM	EPTC	17	Elliptic Functions
PERIOD1.ROM	HTAB	13	(HEPAX RAM only) Periodic Table
41ZL1.ROM	Z4DL	1	41Z Deluxe
ITGDIFF.ROM	FRID	18	Fractional Integro-Differientation
RECURSE.ROM	RCSN	9	Recursion and Modular Math
41ZU1.ROM	Z4DL	4	41Z Deluxe
GAMESB1.ROM	GSB2	16	HP-41 Games Solution Book 1/2

REFERENCES AND INTERESTING WEBSITES.

1. www.hpmuseum.org : the biggest reference site for HP calculators. You can buy its pack with all site contents, with all manuals of any hp calculator known.
2. www.hp41.org : a site completely devoted to the HP41. You can find all modules and manuals
3. www.thecalculatorstore.com : our site, with a specific area for the HP41
4. www.hpcc.org : a British site, Handheld and Portable Computer Club
5. http://www.hp41.net/ : a French site devoted to the HP41C
6. www.systemyde.com : the home of HP41CL
7. Clonix-41 official page by Diego Diaz, creator of the PCB circuit and many other modules and enhancements.
8. La page de Jean-François Garnier (auteur de Emu41) in French
9. HP calculator emulators for the HP calculators by HrastProgrammer
10. Jean-Daniel Dodin, PPC-T
11. La page HP de la maison des Calculatrices Classiques, in French
12. Le HP-41CX sur le site Voidware, in French
13. Le site dédié à la grande famille du HP 41C de Noël Jouenne in French
14. Le site du HP-41CX in French
15. nonpareil HP calculators simulator for Mac OS X
16. Rick Furr's HP calculator page

17. The HP Collection by Matthias Wehrli

---

[i] **Guide to HP Hand Held Calculators and Computers**
W. A. C. Mier Jedrzejowicz

[ii] **Bill & Dave: How Hewlett and Packard Built the World's Greatest Company**
Michael Malone

[iii] HP 41 Service Manual, http://www.thecalculatorstore.com/Manuals/HP41c-service-module-manual_en

[iv] idem

[v] http://www.systemyde.com/pdf/order_fhm_form.pdf

[vi] http://www.thecalculatorstore.com/Zebra-connector-for-HP41C-repair

[vii] https://www.makerspaces.com/how-to-solder/
https://www.howtogeek.com/63630/how-to-use-a-soldering-iron-a-beginners-guide/
https://www.weller-tools.com/how-to-use-soldering-iron/

[viii] https://www.amazon.es/Pasta-de-pulir-cristales-polyWatch/dp/B00E3T237C/ref=sr_1_1?__mk_es_ES=%C3%85M%C3%85%C5%BD%C3%95%C3%91&dchild=1&keywords=polywatch&qid=1590614174&sr=8-1

[ix] Keyboard support for repairs, https://www.thecalculatorstore.com/epages/eb9376.sf/en_GB/?ObjectPath=/Shops/eb9376/Products/%22keyboard%20support%22

[x] Service modules can be found in systemyde.com

[xi] Battery springs can be bought at http://www.thecalculatorstore.com/HP41c-battery-holder-spring

[xii] http://www.systemyde.com/hp41/index.html

[xiii] http://www.systemyde.com/hp41/manuals.html

[xiv] http://www.systemyde.com/hp41/index.html

[xv] 3D Port cover – http://www.thecalculatorstore.com/HP41c-Port-cover-3D

[xvi] 3D Side cover – http://www.thecalculatorstore.com/HP41c-side-cover

[xvii] Battery spring –http://www.thecalculatorstore.com/HP41c-battery-holder-spring

[xviii] 3D Battery holder – http://www.thecalculatorstore.com/Battery-holder-3D